Mary Wilson Alloway

Famous Firesides of French Canada

Mary Wilson Alloway

Famous Firesides of French Canada

ISBN/EAN: 9783337186562

Printed in Europe, USA, Canada, Australia, Japan

Cover: Foto ©ninafisch / pixelio.de

More available books at **www.hansebooks.com**

FAMOUS FIRESIDES

OF

FRENCH CANADA

BY

MARY WILSON ALLOWAY.

ILLUSTRATED.

MONTREAL:
PRINTED BY JOHN LOVELL & SON
1899

Entered according to Act of Parliament of Canada, in the year one thousand eight hundred and ninety-nine, by MARY WILSON ALLOWAY, in the office of the Minister of Agriculture and Statistics at Ottawa.

TO

THE RIGHT HONOURABLE

LORD STRATHCONA AND MOUNT ROYAL, G.C.M.G., LL.D., &c.,

CHANCELLOR OF McGILL UNIVERSITY, MONTREAL,

AND

HIGH COMMISSIONER FOR CANADA IN LONDON,

THIS VOLUME

IS

BY SPECIAL PERMISSION

Respectfully Dedicated

BY

THE AUTHOR.

The principal authorities consulted in the preparation of this work were Le Moyne, Kingsford, Rattray, Garneau, Parkman, Hawkins and Bouchette.

Acknowledgments are also due to the kind interest evinced and encouragement given by the Hon. Judge Baby, President of the Numismatic and Antiquarian Society of Montreal.

CONTENTS

Château de Ramezay	19
Heroes of the Past	30
Chapel of Notre-Dame-de-la-Victoire	51
Le Seminaire	56
Cathedrals and Cloisters	58
Massacre of Lachine	82
Château de Vaudreuil	95
Battle of the Plains	103
Canada under English Rule	125
American Invasion	144
The Continental Army in Canada	155
Fur Kings	192
Interesting Sites	199
Famous Names	203
Echoes from the Past	212

ILLUSTRATIONS.

	PAGE
Fireplace	*Frontispiece.*
Château Kitchen	24
Château de Ramezay	26
Montgomery Salon	28
Chapel of Notre Dame de la Victoire	52
Le Séminaire	56
Home of La Salle	84
St. Amable St	98
Fort Chambly	146
Château Fortier	156
Franklin Vaults	170

PREFACE.

In offering this little volume to the kind consideration of Canadian and American readers, it is the earnest wish of the Author that it may commend itself to the interest of both, as the early histories of Canada and the United States are so closely connected that they may be considered identical.

We have tried to recall the days when, by these firesides, were rocked the cradles of those who helped to make Canadian history, and to render more familiar the names and deeds of the great men, French, English and American, upon whose valour and wisdom such mighty issues depended.

The recital is, we trust, wholly impartial and without prejudice.

It is to be hoped that the union of sentiment which the close of this century sees between the two great Anglo-Saxon peoples may cast a veil of forgetfulness over the strife of the one preceding it; and be a herald of that reign of peace, when " nation shall no more rise against nation, and wars shall cease."

Mary W. Alloway

MONTREAL, May 24, 1899.

INTRODUCTION.

ABOUT twelve years after the first Spanish caravel had touched the shores of North America, we find the French putting forth efforts to share in some of the results of the discovery. In the year 1504 some Basque, Breton and Norman fisherfolk had already commenced fishing along the bleak shores of Newfoundland and the contiguous banks for the cod in which this region is still so prolific.

The Spanish claim to the discovery of America is disputed by several aspirants to that honour. Among these are the ancient mariners of Northern Europe, the Norsemen of the Scandinavian Peninsula. They assert that their Vikings touched American shores three centuries before Isabella of Castille drove the Moors from their palaces among the orange groves of *Espana*. Eric the Red, and other sea-kings, made voyages to Iceland and Greenland in the eleventh and following centuries; and it is highly probable that these Norsemen, with their hardihood and enterprise, touched on some part of the mainland. One Danish writer claims that this occurred as far back as the year 985, about eighty years after the death of the Danes' mortal enemy, the great Saxon King Alfred.

Even the Welsh, from the isolation of their mountain fastnesses, declare that a Cambrian expedition, in the year 1170, under Prince Modoc, landed in America. In proof of this, there is said to exist in Mexico a colony bearing indisputable traces of the tongue of these ancient Celts.

The term Canada first appears as the officially recognized name of the region in the instructions given by Francis I to its original colonists in the year 1538.

There are various theories as to the etymology of the word, its having by different authorities been attributed to Indian, French and Spanish origins.

In an old copy of a Montreal paper, bearing date of Dec. 24, 1834, it is asserted that Canada or *Kannata* is an Indian word, meaning a village, and was mistaken by the early visitors for the name of the whole country.

The Philadelphia *Courier*, of July, 1836, gives the following not improbable etymology of the name of the province :—Canada is compounded of two aboriginal words, *Can*, which signifies the mouth, and *Ada* the country, meaning the mouth of the country. A writer of the same period, when there seems to have been considerable discussion on the subject, says:— The word is undoubtedly of Spanish origin, coming from a common Spanish word, *Canada*, signifying a space or opening between mountains or high banks —a district in Mexico of similar physical features, bearing the same name.

" That there were Spanish pilots or navigators among the first discoverers of the St. Lawrence may be readily supposed, and what more natural than that those who first visited the gulf should call the interior of the country *El Canada* from the typographical appearance of the opening to it, the custom of illiterate navigators naming places from events and natural appearances being well established."

Hennepin, an etymological *savant*, declares that the name arose from the Spaniards, who were the first discoverers of Canada, exclaiming, on their failure to find the precious metals, "*El Capa da nada*," or Cape Nothing. There seems to be some support of this alleged presence of the Spanish among the early navigators of the St. Lawrence, by the finding in the river, near Three Rivers, in the year 1835, an ancient cannon of peculiar make, which was supposed to be of Spanish construction.

The origins of the names of Montreal and Quebec are equally open to discussion. Many stoutly assert that Montreal is the French for Mount Royal, or Royal Mount; others, that by the introduction of one letter, the name is legitimately Spanish—*Monte-real*. *Monte*, designating any wooded elevation, and that *real* is the only word in that language for royal.

The word Quebec is attributed to Indian and French sources. It is said that it is an Algonquin word, meaning a strait, the river at this point being not more than a mile wide; but although Champlain coincided in this view, its root has enver been discovered in any Indian tongue. Its abrupt enunciation has not to the ear the sound of an Indian word, and it could scarcely have come from the Algonquin language, which is singularly soft and sweet, and may be considered the Italian of North American dialects.

Those who claim for it a French origin, say that the Normans, rowing up the river with Cartier at his first discovery, as they rounded the wooded shores of the Isle of Orleans, and came in sight of the bare rock rising three hundred feet from its base, exclaimed "*Quel bec!*" or, What a promontory! The word bears intrinsically strong evidence of Norman origin.

Cape Diamond received its name from the fact that in the "dark colored slate of which it is composed are found perfectly limpid quartz crystals in veins, along with crystallized carbonate of lime, which, sparkling like diamonds among the crags, suggested the appellation."

Famous Firesides
— OF —
French Canada

THE CHATEAU DE RAMEZAY.

A FEW yards from the busy municipal centre of the city of Montreal, behind an antique iron railing, is a quaint, old building known as the Château de Ramezay. Its history is contemporary with that of the city for the last two centuries, and so identified with past stirring events that it has been saved from the vandalism of modern improvement, and is to be preserved as a relic of the old *Régime* in New France. It is a long one-storied structure, originally red-tiled, with graceful, sloping roof, double rows of peaked, dormer windows, huge chimneys and the unpolished architecture of the period.

Among the many historical buildings of America, none have been the scene of more thrilling events, a long line of interesting associations being connected with the now quiet old Château, looking in its peaceful old age as out of keeping with its modern surroundings as would an ancient vellum missal, mellowed for centuries in a monkish cell, appear among some of the ephemeral literature of to-day.

A brilliant line of viceroys have here held rule, and within its walls things momentous in the country's annals have been enacted. During its checkered experience no less than three distinct *Régimes* have followed each other, French, British and American. In an old document still to be found among the archives of the Seminary of St. Sulpice, it is recorded that the land on which it stands was ceded to the Governor of Montreal in the year 1660, just eighteen years after Maisonneuve, its founder, planted the silken Fleur-de-Lys of France on the shores of the savage Redman, and one hundred years before the tri-cross of England floated for the first time from the ramparts.

Somewhere about the year 1700 a portion of this land was acquired by Claude de Ramezay, Sieur de la Gesse, Bois Fleurent and Monnoir, in France, and Governor of Three Rivers, and this house built.

De Ramezay was of an old Franco-Scottish family, being descended by *Thimothy*, his father, from one Sir John Ramsay, a Scotchman, who, with others of his compatriots, went over to France in the 16th century. He may have joined an army raised for the French wars, or may have formed part of a bridal train similar to the gay retinue of the fair Princess Mary, who went from the dark fells and misty lochs of the land of the Royal Stuarts to be the loveliest queen who ever sat on the throne of *la belle France*. De Ramezay was the father of thirteen children, by his wife, Mademoiselle Denys de la Ronde, a sister of Mesdames Thomas Tarieu de La Naudière de La Pérade, d'Ailleboust d'Argenteuil, Chartier de Lotbinière and Aubert de la Chenage, the same family out of whom came the celebrated de Jumonville, so well known in connection with the unfortunate circumstances of Fort Necessity. The original of the marriage contract is still preserved in the records of the Montreal Court House; with its long list of autographs of Governor, Intendant, and high officials, civil and military, scions of the nobility of the country, appended thereto. The annals of the family tell us that some of them died in infancy, several met violent and untimely deaths, two of the sisters took conventual vows in the cloisters of Quebec, two married, having descendants now living in France and Canada, and two remained unmarried.

De Ramezay came over as a captain in the army with the Viceroy de Tracy, and was remarkable for his highly refined education, having been a pupil of the celebrated Fénélon, who was said to have been the pattern of virtue in the midst of a corrupt court, and who was entrusted by Louis the Fourteenth with the education of his grandsons, the Dukes of Burgundy, Anjou and Berri. Had the first named, who was heir-presumptive to the throne, lived to practice the princely virtues, the seeds of which his preceptor had sown in his heart, some of the most bloody pages in French history might never have been written.

De Ramezay, for many years being Governor of Montreal, held official court in the Council chamber to the right of the entrance hall of the Château, which is now a museum of rare and valuable relics of Canada's past.

The Salon was the scene of many a gay rout, as Madame de Ramezay, imitating the brilliant social and political life as it was in France in the time of *Le Grand Monarque*, transplanted to the wilds of America some reflection of court ceremonial and display as they culminated in that long and brilliant reign. From the dormer windows above, high-bred French ladies looked at the sun rising over the forest-clothed shores of the river, on which now stands the architectural grandeur of the modern city. How strange to the swarthy-faced dwellers in the wigwam must the old-time gaieties have appeared, as the lights from the silver *candelabres* shone far out in the night, when the old Château was *en fête* and aglow with music, dancing and laughter.

What a contrast to the burden-bearing squaws were the dainty French women in stiff brocade and jewels, high heels, paint, patches and tresses *à la Pompadour*, tripping through the stately measures of the minuet to the sound of lute or harpsichord!

> "O, fair young land of *La Nouvelle France*,
> With thy halo of olden time romance,
> Back like a half-forgotten dream
> Come the bygone days of the old *Régime*."

The servants and retainers, imitating their lords, held high revel in the vaulted kitchens; while dishes and confections, savoury and delicious, came from the curious fire-place and ovens recently discovered in the vaults. These ancient kitchen offices, built to resist a siege, are exceedingly interesting in the light of our culinary arrangements of to-day. They were so constructed that if the buildings above, with their massive masonry, were destroyed, they would afford safe and comfortable refuge. The roof is arched, and, like the walls, is several feet thick, of solid stone,

lighted by heavily barred windows, with strong iron shutters. In clearing out the walled-up and long-forgotten ovens, there were found bits of broken crockery, pipe-stems and the ashes of fires, gone out many, many long years ago. As indicated by an early map of the city, the position of the original well was located; in which, when it is cleaned out, it is intended to hang an old oaken bucket and drinking cups as nearly as possible as they originally were.

Some time after the death of de Ramezay, which occurred in the city of Quebec in 1724, these noble halls fell into the possession of the fur-traders of Canada, and many a time these underground cellars were stored with the rich skins of the mink, silver fox, marten, sable and ermine for the markets of Europe and for royalty itself. They were brought in by the hunters and trappers over the boundless domains of the fur companies, and by the Indian tribes friendly to the peltrie trade. As these hardy, bronzed men sat around the hearth, while the juicy haunch of venison roasted on the spit by the blazing logs, relating blood-curdling tales and hair-breadth escapes, they were a necessary phase of times long passed away, but which will always have a picturesqueness especially their own.

Instead of the white man's influencing the savage towards civilized customs, it was often found, as one writer has said, that hundreds of white men were barbarized on this continent for each single savage that was civilized. Many of the former identified themselves by marriage and mode of life with the Indians, developed their traits of hardihood and acquired their knowledge of woodcraft and skill in navigating the streams. In pursuit of the fur-bearing animals in their native haunts, they shot the raging rapids, ventured out upon the broad expanse of the treacherous lakes, and endured without complaint the severity of winter and the exposure of forest life in summer.

Their ranks were continually increased by those who were impatient of the slow method of obtaining a livelihood from the tillage of the soil, when the husbandman

CHATEAU DE RAMEZAY.

was frequently driven from the plough by the sudden attack of Indian foes, or interrupted in his hasty and anxious harvesting by their war-whoop, or perhaps was compelled to leave his farm to take up arms, if the occasion arose, so that in many instances the homesteads were left to the old men, women and children. The excitement of the chase and the wild freedom of the plains had a fascination that many could not resist, so much so that the king had to promulgate an edict, to stop, under heavy penalties, this roving life of his Canadian subjects, as their nomadic tendencies interfered with the successful settlement of the colony.

To the lover of the quaint architecture of other centuries, there is an indescribable charm in these time-worn walls, which are still as substantial as if the snows and rains of two centuries had not beaten against them. The interior is equally interesting in this regard, as the walls dividing the chambers and corridors, though covered with modern plaster and stucco, are found to consist of several feet of solid stone masonry, while the ornamental ceiling covers beams of timber, twenty inches by eighteen, which is strong, well jointed and placed as close as flooring. Above this is heavy stone work over twelve inches thick, so that the sloping roof was the only part pregnable in an assault with the munitions of war then in use. Upon removing a portion of the modern wainscotting in the main reception room, there was discovered an ancient fireplace, made of roughly hewn blocks of granite. A crescent-shaped portion of the hearthstone is capable of removal, for what purpose it is not known. With old andirons and huge logs, it looks to-day exactly as it must have done when Montgomery and his suite, in revolutionary uniform, received delegations in this chamber, and when Brigadier General Wooster, who succeeded him, wrote and sent despatches by courier from the French Château to the Colonial mansion at Mount Vernon.

The rooms of state in those days were, it is said, all in what is at present the back of the house, the rear of the building being

COPYRIGHT.   Salon in which Montgomery held official receptions, 1775.

the front, facing the river, down to which ran the gardens.

It may be that the moonlight cast on these panes the shadow of the noble Sir Jeffrey Amherst, in his red coat, as looking out over the river he may have seen the smoke of the fire lighted by de Lévis, where he burnt his colours rather than let them fall into the hands of the English.

HEROES OF THE PAST.

ON the river bank below the Château, tradition says, was the spot trodden by Jacques Cartier, who gave the river its name. Born at the time when all Europe was still excited over the tales of Columbus' adventures, he left the white cliffs and grey docks of St. Malo, where he had learned the sailor's craft, to search for the western route to the Indies.

A little higher up, less than a century later, Champlain, to push on actively his operations in the fur-trade, built his fort, the name which he then gave the spot, "*Place Royale*," being recently restored to it. In his wanderings for the further pursuance of this object, he discovered Lakes Ontario, Huron and Champlain.

Being betrothed to a twelve year old maiden, Hélène Bouillé, the daughter of a Huguenot, he named the island opposite the city, which lies like a green gem among the crystal waters, Hélène, in affectionate remembrance of her who, at the end of eight years, was to join him in his adventurous life.

The winding length of quiet, old St. Paul street, then an Indian trail, following the course of the river through the oak forest, must often have known the presence of this picturesque warrior in his weather-beaten garments of the doublet and long hose then in vogue. "Over the doublet he buckled on a breastplate, and probably a back piece, while his thighs were protected by cuisses of steel and his head by a plumed casque. Across his shoulders hung the strap of his *baudolier* or ammunition box, at his side was his sword, and in his hand his arquebuse. Such was the equipment of this ancient Indian fighter, whose exploits date eleven years before the Puritans landed," among the grey granite hills of New England.

He was an armourer of Dieppe, who, though "a great captain, a successful discoverer and a noted geographer, was more than all a God-fearing, Christian gentleman." He was more concerned to gain victories by the cross than by the sword, saying:—"The salvation of a soul is of more value than the conquest of an empire."

The year 1620 was a red letter day in the history of the Colony, when, from a little vessel moored at the foot of the cliff, he led on shore at Quebec his young bride, who with her three maids had come to the western wilderness, the first gentlewoman to land on Canadian shores. He conducted her to where is now the corner of Notre Dame and Sous-le-Fort streets, to the rude "*habitation*" he had prepared for her reception, which was poorly furnished and unhomelike in comparison to the one which she had left over the sea. But history tells of no word of complaint nor disappointment coming from the gentle lips; but, as the youthful *châteleine* sat by her hearth, it shed a light among the huts of the settlers and dusky lodges of the natives, as her example of patience and duty performed by the first refined, civilized fireside in the land does to the thousands who have succeeded her. After almost three hundred years, the "charms of her person, her elegance and kindliness of manner" are still remembered. The chronicler tells us that the "Governor's lady wore in her daily rambles, amongst the wigwams, an article of feminine attire, not unusual in those days, a small mirror at her girdle. It appealed irresistibly to the simple natures around her, that "a beauteous being should love them so much as to carry their images reflected close to her heart."

"The graceful figure of the first lady of Canada, gliding noiselessly along by the murmuring waters of the St. Lawrence, showering everywhere smiles and kindness, a help-mate to her noble lord, and a pattern of purity and refinement, was indeed a vision of female loveliness" which time cannot obliterate nor forgetfulness dim. The domestic life of the colony dates from about the time of her arrival, the first regular register of marriage being entered in the following year; two months after the first nuptial ceremony was performed in New England. The first christening took place in the same year, 1621, the ordinance being administered to the infant son of Abraham Martin, *di^t L'Ecossais*, pilot of the river St. Lawrence. This old pilot, named in the journal of the Jesuits as *Maître* Abraham, has bequeathed his name to the famous Plains, on which was decided the destiny of New France.

It was indeed a sorry day for the settlement when the inhabitants, on the 16th of August, 1624, saw the white sails of Champlain's vessel disappear behind what is now Point Levis, carrying back, alas! forever, to the shores of her beloved France, Madame de Champlain, sighing for the mystic life of the cloister, tired out by the incessant alarms and the Indian ferocities spread around the Fort during the frequent absences of her husband and her favourite brother, Eustache Bouillé." The daintily-nurtured French lady must have found the quiet of the old-world convent a very haven of peace and rest. She died at Mieux, an

Ursuline Nun, in the order which subsequently was to be so closely identified with the religious history of her wilderness home.

But monastic retreat had no attractions for the founder of Fort St. Louis. Parkman says : "Champlain, though in Paris is restless. He is enamoured of the New World, whose rugged charms have seized his fancy and his heart. His restless thoughts revert to the fog-wrapped coasts, the piney odours of the forests, the noise of waters and the sharp and piercing sunlight so dear to his remembrance."

Among these he was destined to lay down his well worn armour at the command of death, the only enemy before whom he ever retreated ; for on Christmas Day, 1635, in a chamber in the Fort at Quebec, "breathless and cold lay the hardy frame which war, the wilderness and the sea had buffeted so long in vain. The chevalier, crusader, romance-loving explorer and practical navigator lay still in death," leaving the memory of a courage that was matchless and a patience that was sublime.

For over two hundred and sixty years, no monument stood to celebrate this true patriot's name, but now his statue stands in his city, near to where he laid the foundations and built the Château St. Louis. Most unfortunately his last resting place is unknown, notwithstanding the laborious and learned efforts of the many distinguished antiquarians of Quebec.

The Fort which Champlain built in 1620, and in which he died, was for over two centuries the seat of government, and the name recalls the thrilling events which clothed it with an atmosphere of great and stirring interest during its several periods. The hall of the Fort during the weakness of the colony was often, it is said, a scene of terror and despair from the inroads of the ferocious savages, who, having passed and overthrown all the French outposts, threatened the Fort itself, and massacred some friendly Indians within sight of its walls.

"In the palmy days of French sovereignty it was the centre of power over the immense domain extending from the Gulf of St. Lawrence along the shores of the noble river and down the course of the Mississippi to its outlet below New Orleans.

The banner which first streamed from the battlements of Quebec was displayed from a line of forts which protected the settlements throughout this vast extent of country. The Council Chamber of the Castle was the scene of many a midnight vigil, many a long deliberation and deep-laid project, to free the continent from the intrusion of the ancient rivals of France and assert her supremacy. Here also was rendered, with all its ancient forms, the fealty and homage of the *noblesse* and military retainers, who held possessions under the Crown, a feudal service suited to those early times, and which is still performed by the peers at the coronation of our kings in Westminster Abbey."

Among the many dramatic scenes of

which it was the theatre, no occurrence was more remarkable than an event which happened in the year 1690, when "Castle St. Louis had assumed an appearance worthy of the Governor-General, who then made it the seat of the Royal Government, the dignified Count de Frontenac,

a nobleman of great talents, long service and extreme pride, and who is considered one of the most illustrious of the early French rulers." The story is, that Sir William Phipps, an English admiral, arriving with his fleet in the harbour, and believing the city to be in a defenceless condition, thought he might capture it by surprise. An officer was sent ashore with a flag of truce. He was met half way by a French major and his men, who, placing a bandage over the intruder's eyes, conducted him by a circuitous route to the Castle, having recourse on the way to various stratagems, such as making small bodies of soldiers cross and re-cross his path, to give him the impression of the presence of a strong force. On arriving at the Castle, his surprise we are told was extreme on finding himself in the presence of the Governor-General, the Intendant and the Bishop, with a large staff of French officers, uniformed in full regimentals, drawn up in the centre of the great hall ready to receive him.

The British officer immediately handed to Frontenac a written demand for an unconditional surrender, in the name of the new Sovereigns, William and Mary, whom Protestant England had crowned instead of the dethroned and Catholic James. Taking his watch from his pocket and placing it on a table near by, he peremptorily demanded a positive answer in an hour's time at the furthest. This action was like the spark in the tinder, and completely roused the anger and indignation of his hearers, who had scarcely been able to restrain their excitement during the reading of the summons, which the Englishman had delivered in an imperious voice, and which an interpreter had translated word for word to the outraged audience.

A murmur of repressed resentment ran through the assembly, when one of the officers, without waiting for his superior to reply, exclaimed impetuously:—that the messenger ought to be treated as the envoy of a corsair, or common marauder, since Phipps was in arms against his legitimate Sovereign. Frontenac, although keenly hurt in his most vulnerable point, —his pride—by the lack of ceremony displayed in the conduct of the Englishman, replied in a calm voice, but in impassioned words, saying loftily:—" You will have no occasion to wait so long for my answer,—here it is :—I do not recognize King William, but I know that the Prince of Orange is an usurper, who has violated the most sacred ties of blood and religion in dethroning the King, his father-in-law; and I acknowledge no other legitimate Sovereign than James the Second. Do your best, and I will do mine."

The messenger thereupon demanded that the reply be given him in writing, which the Governor haughtily refused, saying :—

" I am going to answer your master at the cannon's mouth ; he shall be taught that this is not the manner in which a person of my rank ought to be summoned."

Charlevoix seems to have very much admired the lordly bearing of Frontenac on this occasion, which was so trying to his self-control, but, with an impartiality creditable to a Frenchman, he justly chronicles his equal admiration for the coolness and presence of mind with which the Englishman signalized himself in carrying out his mission, under insults and humiliations scarcely to be looked for from those who should have known better the respect due to a flag of truce.

The commander of the fleet, finding the place ready for resistance, concluded that the lateness of the season rendered it unwise to commence a regular siege against a city whose natural and artificial defences made it a formidable fortress, and which, when garrisoned by troops of such temper and mettle, it appeared impossible to reduce. It must also be considered that Phipps had been delayed by contrary winds and pilots ignorant of the river navigation, which combination of untoward circumstances conspired to compel him to relinquish his design, which under more favouring conditions he might have carried out with success, and conquered the place before it could have been known in Montreal that it was even in danger.

"Without doubt Frontenac was the most conspicuous figure which the annals of the early colonization of Canada affords. He was the descendant of several generations of distinguished men who were famous as courtiers and soldiers." He was of Basque origin and proud of his noble ancestry. He was born in 1620, and was distinguished by becoming the god-child of the King, the royal sponsor bestowing his own name on the unconscious babe, who was in after years to be a sturdy defender of France's dominions over the ocean. He became a soldier at the age of fifteen, and even in early youth and manhood saw active service and gave promise of gallantry and bravery.

In October, 1648, he married the lovely young Anne de la Grange-Trianon, a "maiden of imperious temper, lively wit and marvellous grace." She was a beauty of the court and chosen friend of Mademoiselle de Montpensier, the granddaughter of King Henry the Fourth. A celebrated painting of the *Comtesse de*

Frontenac, in the character of Minerva, smiles on the walls of one of the galleries at Versailles.

The marriage took place without the consent of the bride's relatives, and soon proved an ill-starred one, the young wife's fickle affection turning into a strong repulsion for her husband, whom she intrigued to have sent out of the country.

Her influence at court, and some jealousy on the part of the King combined to bring about this end, and Frontenac was appointed Governor and Lieutenant-General of *La Nouvelle France*.

Parkman says:—" A man of courts and camps, born and bred in the focus of a most gorgeous civilization, he was banished to the ends of the earth, among savage hordes and half-reclaimed forests, to exchange the splendour of St. Germain and the dawning glories of Versailles for a stern, grey rock, haunted by sombre priests, rugged merchants, traders, blanketed Indians and wild bushrangers." When he sailed up the river and the stern grandeur of the scene opened up before him, he felt as he afterwards wrote:—

"I never saw anything more superb than the position of this town. It could not be better situated for the future capital of an empire."

But the dainty and luxurious *Comtesse* had no taste for pioneer life, and no thought of leaving her silken-draped *boudoir* for a home in a rude fort on a rock; she therefore accepted the offer of a domicile with her kindred spirit, Mademoiselle d'Outrelaise. The "*Divines*," as they were called, established a *Salon*, which, among the many similar coteries of the time, was remarkable for its wit and gaiety. It set the fashion to French society, and was affected by all the leading spirits of the Court and Capital.

Although an occasional *billet* came from the recreant spouse to her husband in the Castle St. Louis, no home life nor welcoming domestic fire-side threw a charm over his exile. The glamour with which affection can glorify even the rudest surroundings was denied him in his long life of seventy-six years.

To avoid the confusion to which the

terms Fort St. Louis and Castle St. Louis might lead, it must be understood that they in a measure were the same, as the one enclosed the other.

In the year 1834, two hundred and fourteen years after the foundation of this Chateau, a banquet was prepared for the reception of those invited to partake of the official hospitality of the Governor; when suddenly the tocsin sounded,—the dreaded alarm of fire. Soon the streets were thronged with citizens, with anxious enquiries passing from lip to lip, and ere long the cry was uttered: " To the Castle, to the Castle ! "

The entire population of merchants and artisans, soldiers from the garrison, priests from the monasteries, and citizens, rich and poor, joined hands with the firemen to save the mediæval fortress from destruction, and its treasured contents from the flames. Old silver was snatched from the banquet table by some who had expected to sit around the board as guests.

At the head of the principal staircase, where it had stood for fifty years or more, was a bust of Wolfe, with the inscription upon it:—

"Let no vain tear upon this bust be shed,
A common tribute to the common dead,
But let the good, the generous, the brave,
With God-like envy sigh for such a grave."

Fortunately, in the confusion of the disaster it was not overlooked, but was carried to a place of safety. While every heart present could not but be moved with the deepest feelings of regret at the loss of its hoary walls, yet the beholder was forced to admire the magnificent spectacular effect of the conflagration which crowned the battlements and reflected over crag and river, as the old fort, which had stubbornly resisted all its enemies during five sieges, fell before the devouring element.

Its stones were permeated with the military and religious history of the "old rock city," for, in the fifteen years of its occupancy by Champlain, it was as much a mission as a fort. The historian says:—
"A stranger visiting the Fort of Quebec would have been astonished at its air of conventual decorum. Black-robed Jesuits

and scarfed officers mingled at Champlain's table. There was little conversation, but in its place histories and the lives of the saints were read aloud, as in a monastic refectory. Prayers, masses and confessions followed each other, and the bell of the adjacent chapel rang morning, noon and night. Quebec became a shrine. Godless soldiers whipped themselves to penitence, women of the world outdid each other in the fury of their contrition, and Indians gathered thither for the gifts of kind words and the polite blandishments bestowed upon them."

The site where the old Château St. Louis once stood, with its halo of romance and renown, is now partially covered by the great Quebec hostelry, the Château Frontenac, which in its erection and appointments has not destroyed, but rather perpetuated, the traditions of the " Sentinel City of the St. Lawrence."

" Château Frontenac has been planned with the strong sense of the fitness of things, being a veritable old-time Château, whose curves and cupolas, turrets and towers, even whose tones of gray stone and dulled brick harmonize with the sober quaint architecture of our dear old Fortress City, and looks like a small bit of Mediæval Europe perched upon a rock."

Under the promenade of Durham Terrace is still the cellar of the old Château; and standing upon it, the patriot, whether English or French, cannot but thrill as he looks on the same scene upon which the heroes of the past so often gazed, and from which they flung defiance to their foes.

On almost the same spot upon which Champlain had landed at Montreal, and about seven years after his death, a small band of consecrated men and women, singing a hymn, drew up their tempest-worn pinnace, and raised their standard in the name of King Louis, while Maisonneuve, the ascetic knight, planted a crucifix, and dedicated the land to God.

The city as it stands on this spot is a fulfilment of his vow then made, when he declared, as he pitched his tent and lighted his camp-fire, that here he would found a city though every tree on the island were an Iroquois. On an altar of bark, decorated with wild flowers and lighted by fireflies, the first mass was celebrated, and the birthnight of Montreal registered.

From the little seed thus planted in this rude altar, a mighty harvest has arisen in cathedral, monastery, church and convent, representing untold wealth and influence. The early French explorer, with a "sword in his hand and a crucifix on his breast," was more desirous of Christianizing than of conquering the native tribes. So completely has this creed become identified with the country's character and history, that the province of Quebec is emphatically a Catholic community. So faithfully have its tenets been handed down by generations of devout followers of this faith, that even the streets and squares bear the names of saints and martyrs, such as St. Francis Xavier, St. Peter, St. John, St. Joseph, St. Mary, and in fact the entire calendar is represented, especially in the east end of the town. St. Paul, which was probably the first street laid out, is called after the city's founder himself,—Paul Chomedy de Maisonneuve.

NOTRE-DAME-DE-LA-VICTOIRE.

A FEW rods to the west of the Château, through a vaulted archway leading from the street, in the shadow of the peaceful convent buildings is a little chapel called *Notre-Dame-de-la-Victoire*. The swallows twittering under its broken eaves are now the only sign of life; and its rotting timbers and threshold, forgotten by the world, give no suggestion of the martial incident to which it owes its existence. While the American Colonies were still English, the British Ensign floated over Boston town, and good Queen Anne was prayed for in Puritan pulpits, an expedition was fitted out under Sir Hovenden Walker to drive the French out of Canada. In the previous year, 1710, the Legislature of New York had taken steps to lay before the Queen the alarming progress of Gallic domination in America, saying:—

" It is well known that the French can

go by water from Quebec to Montreal; from thence they can do the like through the rivers and lakes, at the risk of all your Majesty's plantations on this Continent, as far as Carolina."

In the command of Walker were several companies of regulars draughted from the great Duke of Marlborough's Army. While he was leading it from victory to victory for the glory of his King, his wife, the famous Sarah Jennings, was making a conquest at home of the affections of the simple-minded and susceptible Queen. It is remarkable that the coronet of this ambitious woman should now rest on the brow of an American girl, and that a daughter of New York should reign at Blenheim Castle. At that period France possessed the two great valleys of North America, the Mississippi and the St. Lawrence; to capture the latter was the aim of the expedition.

As the hostile fleet sailed up the St. Lawrence, a storm of great severity burst upon the invaders. Eight of the transports were recked on the reefs, and in the dawn

CHAPEL OF NOTRE-DAME-DE-LA-VICTOIRE.

of the midsummer morning the bodies of a thousand red-coated soldiers were strewn on the sands of *Isle-aux-Œufs*. It has been said that an old sea-dog, Jean Paradis, refused to act as pilot, and in a fog allowed them to run straight on to death; and also that among those who perished was one of the court beauties who had eloped with Sir Hovenden

The disabled vessels retreated before the artillery of the elements, and left Bourbon's Lilied Blue to wave for half a century longer over Fort St. Louis. This bloodless victory for the French was attributed by them to the intervention of the Virgin, in gratitude for which this chapel was vowed and built, as was also another on the market place, Lower Town, Quebec. The miraculous feature of the defeated invasion was considered certain from the fact that a recluse in the convent near the chapel, and who was remarkable for her piety, had embroidered a prayer to the Virgin on the flag which the Baron de Longueuil had borne from Montreal in command of a detachment of troops.

Some of the original interior fittings of the chapel still exist, but the bell which chimed its first call to vespers, when the great city was a quiet, frontier hamlet, has long been silent. It is to be regretted that from its historical character it has not been preserved from decay, but looks as time-worn and mouldering as does the rusty cannon in the hall of the Château, which was one of the guns of the ill-fated fleet, and over which the river had flowed for almost two hundred years. Seven of England's sovereigns had lived, reigned and died, and in France the Royal house had fallen in the deluge of blood that flowed around the guillotine. Quebec had changed flags—the Tri-color had been unfurled over the *Hotel-de-Ville* at Paris, and the Stars and Stripes over the new-born nation.

The thrones of Europe had tottered at the word of the Corsican boy,—he had played with crowns as with golden baubles, and had gone from the imperial purple to the mist-shrouded rocks of St. Helena. Eugenie, the Beautiful, had ruled the world by her grace, and fled from the throne of the haughty Louis to a loveless exile—while the old gun, with its charge rusting in its mouth, lay in silence under the passing keels of a million craft.

LE SÉMINAIRE.

STILL more ancient is a venerable postern in the blackened wall of the Seminary of St. Sulpice, near by, which is now the oldest building in the city, being erected some fifty years before the Château. It leads by a narrow lane to the gardens of the Monastery, which bloom quiet and still here in the heart of the throbbing life of a city of to-day. Generations of saintly men, under vows, have trodden in the shade of its walks, trying with the rigours of monastic life to crush out the memories of love and home left behind among the sun-kissed vineyards of France. For two hundred years and more no woman's footstep had fallen here among the flowers, until recently the wife of a Governor-General was admitted on a special occasion. On the cobble-stones of the courtyard, pilgrims, penitents, priests and soldiers have trodden, the echoes of their footsteps passing away in centuries of years. Above the walls, blackened by time and pierced by windows

SEMINARY OF ST. SULPICE

with the small panes of a fashion gone by, the bells of the clock ring out the stroke of midnight over one-third of a million souls, as it did the hours of morning when the great-great-grandfathers of the present generation ran to school over the grass-grown pavements of young Ville-Marie.

"The inimitable old roof-curves still cover the walls, and the Fleur-de-Lys still cap the pinnacles" as in the days when Richelieu, the prince of prelates, sought to plant the feudalism and Christianity of old France on the shores of the new. They still rise against the blue of Canadian skies unmolested, while in France, in the early years of the century, popular frenzy dragged this symbol of royalty from the spires of the churches and convents of Paris.

CATHEDRALS AND CLOISTERS.

THE Order of the Gentlemen of St. Sulpice is supposed to be very rich, the amount of the immense revenues never being made public. They were the feudal lords of the Island of Montreal in the earlier chapters of its history. Through their zealous efforts and the generosity of their parishioners was opened in the year eighteen hundred and twenty-nine the grand church adjoining, that of *Notre Dame*, built on the site of the original parish church. Viewing it from the extensive *plaza* in front, its imposing proportions fill the beholder with the same awe as when looking at some lofty mountain peak, but its symmetry is so exquisite that its size cannot at first be appreciated.

In imitation of its prototype, *Notre Dame de Paris*, twin towers rise in stateliness to a height of two hundred and twenty-seven feet, and are visible for a distance of thirty miles. The façade is impressive, the style a modification of different schools adapted to carry out the design intended. Three colossal statues of the Virgin, St. Joseph and St. John the Baptist are placed over the arcades. The sublime structure belongs to a branch of the Gothic, in the pointed arch type of architecture which was brought home from the Crusades,—a style which has come down from the time-honoured architecture of the old world, when religious thought that now finds expression in books was written and symbolized in stone.

From a vestibule at the foot of the western tower, an ascent of two hundred and seventy-nine steps offers a most enchanting view of mountain, river, street and harbour, with such a wilderness of dome, steeple and belfry, that the exclamation involuntarily arises—this is truly a city of churches!

On the descent, a pause on a platform gives the opportunity of admiring "*Le Gros Bourdon*," or great bell, and one of the largest in the world. It weighs twenty-four thousand, seven hundred and eighty pounds, and is six feet high. Its mouth measures eight feet, seven inches in diameter. The tone is magnificent in depth and fullness. On occasions such as the death of high ecclesiastics or other solemn events, its tolling is indescribable in its slow, sonorous vibrations. In the eastern tower hang ten smaller bells of beautiful quality, and so harmonized that choice and varied compositions can be performed by the eighteen ringers required in their manipulation. On high festivals, when all ring out with brazen tongues, caught up and re-echoed from spire to spire in what Victor Hugo describes as:—" Mingling and blending in the air like a rich embroidery of all sorts of melodious sounds " —America can furnish no greater oratorio.

Its interior, which is profusely embellished and enriched, the spacious, two-storied galleries, in a twilight of mysterious gloom, and an altar upon which so much wealth has been consecrated, combine to make it a temple worthy of any time or race.

"Whatever may be the external differences, we always find in the Christian Cathedral, no matter how modified, the Roman Basilica. It rises forever from the ground in harmony with the same laws. There are invariably two naves intersecting each other in the form of a cross, the upper end being rounded into a chancel or choir. There are always side aisles for processions or for chapels, and a sort of lateral gallery into which the principal nave opens by means of the spaces between the columns.

" The number of chapels, steeples, doors and spires may be modified indefinitely, according to the century, the people and the art. Statues, stained glass, rose-windows, arabesques, denticulations, capitals and bas-reliefs are employed according as they are desired. Hence the immense variety in the exterior of structures, within which there dwells such unity and order."

The nave here is two hundred and twenty feet long, almost eighty in height, and one hundred and twenty in width, including the side aisles. The walls, which are five feet thick, have fourteen side windows forty feet high, which light softly the galleries and grand aisle. So admirable is the arrangement, that fifteen thousand people can find accommodation and hear perfectly in all parts of the building. On high festivals, such as Christmas or Easter, when the great organ, said to be the finest in America, under the fingers of a master, with full choir and orchestra, rolls out the music of the masses, the senses are enthralled by the magnificence of the harmony. The various altars and mural decorations are beautiful with painting, gilding and carving. In the subdued light, which filters through the stained windows, are found many things of especial sanctity to the faithful. On a column rests an exquisite little statuette of the Virgin, which was a gift from Pope Pius the Ninth, the finely chased and wrought crucifix and the riband attached to it having been worn around the neck of the High Pontiff himself. Directly opposite to it is a statue of St. Peter, a copy of that at Rome. Fifty days indulgence are granted to those who piously kiss this image. Under one altar rest the bones of St. Felix, which were taken from the Catacombs at Rome, and on another is a picture of the Madonna, said to be a copy of one painted by St. Luke. On all the shrines are candlesticks, votive offerings and many other articles of great age, value and veneration.

The main altar is exceedingly rich in artistic ornamentation, representing in its design the religious history of the world, and is the only one of the kind in existence. Although the foundation stones of this great pile were laid seventy years ago, this grand anthem in stone has not yet reached its "amen," many additions to it being yet in contemplation.

Like many others of earth masterpieces in architecture, it is at once the monument to and the mausoleum of its builder, whose body, according to his dying request, although a Protestant, lies in the vaults beneath his greatest life-work.

Through some halls and corridors back of the grand altar is the chapel of "Our

Lady of the Sacred Heart," which is one of the most beautiful sanctuaries in the city, and remarkable for the harmony of its lines and proportions. It is in the form of a cross, ninety feet in length, eighty-five feet in the transept with an altitude of fifty-five feet. The splendour of its ornamentation, carving, sculpture, elegant galleries, panels in mosaic, original paintings by Canadian artists, and a beautiful reproduction of Raphael's celebrated frieze of "The Dispute of the Blessed Sacrament," unite to constitute this piece of ecclesiastical architecture a *chef d'œuvre*.

An iconoclast might marvel at the absorption in prayer of some of the devotees, among accessories bewildering to eyes accustomed to the plainer surroundings of other forms of ritual, but the worship of those in attendance seems sincere and complete.

Following the footsteps of Cartier to where, near the foot of Mount Royal, he found the Indian village of Hochelaga, is now to be seen the St. James' Cathedral, which is a reduced copy of St. Peter's at Rome, the great centre from which radiates the Catholicism of Christendom. It is somewhat less than half the dimensions of its model, with certain modifications necessary in the differences of climate. The work was entrusted to M. Victor Bourgeau, who, to gain the information necessary to carry out successfully a repetition of the great master, Michael Angelo's conception, spent some time in the Eternal City studying the various details. But the real architect, it may be said, who made the plans and supervised and directed the building of the sacred monument, was Rev. Father Michaud, of the St. Viateur Order. To raise the funds necessary for the initial work, every member of the immense diocese was taxed; and even now, after a lapse of thirty years, it is still unfinished, so great has been the expense involved. The handsome façade is elaborately columned in cut-stone, for which only blocks of the most perfect kind were used.

Like the colossal dome at Rome, this one towers above every other structure in the city, with the height of the cross included, being forty feet higher than the lofty towers of *Notre Dame*. It is seventy feet in diameter, and two hundred and ten feet above the pavement. It is after the work of Brunelleschi, whose exquisite art and genius flung the airy grace of his incomparable domes against Florentine and Roman skies.

There is none of the "dim, religious light" in the interior decoration of white and gold, the subtle colouring of the symbolic frescoing and the brilliance of the gold and brazen altar furnishing. At a service celebrated especially for the Papal Zuaves, the picturesque red and grey of their uniform, the priests in gorgeous canonicals of scarlet, stiff with gold, the acolytes in white surplices and the venerable archbishop in cardinal and purple, with a chorus from Handel ringing through the vaulted roof, a full conception of the Papal form of worship can be obtained; while a squaw in blanket and moccasins kneeling on the floor beside a fluted pillar seems the living symbol of the heathendom the early fathers came to convert.

In Canada the Jesuits have always been prominent in its history, signalizing themselves by extraordinary devotion and self-sacrifice, and were among the earliest explorers of the Continent, the first sound of civilization over many of the lakes and rivers being the chant of the capuchined friar. Fathers Brebœuf and Lalemant, burnt by the Indians; Garreau, butchered; Chabanel, drowned by an apostate Huron, and others hideously tortured, testified with their blood to their devotion. From the Atlantic to the prairies, from the bleak shores of the Hudson Bay to the sunny beaches of Louisiana, they suffered, bled and died.

It is said the Jesuits have a genius for selecting sites, and certainly the situation of their especial church and adjoining colleges bears out the statement. Like the other churches of this most Catholic city, it is not complete, the towers having yet to be continued into spires. It is much frequented for the fine music and admired for its beautiful interior. It is in the Florentine Renaissance style, which is the one usually favoured by this Order. The frescoes are unusually pleasing, being in soft tones of monochrome, the work of eminent Roman artists, and are reproductions of the modern German School of Biblical scenes and from the history of the Jesuits. There are in addition some fine paintings by the Gagliardi brothers at Rome and others.

In the Eastern part of the city, commonly called the French quarter, so purely French are the people, with temperaments as gay and volatile as in *Le Beau Paris* itself, is a gem of architecture in the church of " Our Lady of Lourdes." This chapel, reared as a visible expression of the dogma of the Immaculate Conception, is of the Byzantine and Renaissance type, a style frequently to be seen reflected from the lagoons of Venice.

" The choir and transepts terminate in a circular domed apsis, and a large central dome rises at the intersection of the latter. The statue over the altar, and which immediately strikes the eye, is symbolic of the doctrine illustrated. The Virgin is represented in the attitude usually shown in the Spanish School of Painters, with hands crossed upon the breast, standing on a cloud with the words : 'A woman clothed with the sun and the moon under her feet.'" A singularly beautiful light, thrown down from an unseen source, casts a kind of heavenly radiance around the figure with fine effect.

"Some of the painting is exceedingly good. The decoration of the church, in gold and colours, arabesque and fifteenth century ornament, is very beautiful and harmonious. This building is interesting as being the only one of the kind in America."

By descending a narrow stairway, which winds beneath the floor, is found a shrine fitted up in imitation of the grotto near Lourdes, in France, in which it is said the Virgin appeared to a young girl, Bernadette Souberous, at which time a miracle-working fountain is said to have gushed out of the rock, and still continues its wonderful cures. A goblet of the water stands on the altar, and is said to have powers of healing. This underground shrine, lighted only by dim, coloured lamps, gives a sensation of peculiar weirdness after the light and beauty of the structure above.

Perhaps there is no church of French Canada of deeper interest than " *Notre*

Dame de Bonsecours." On its site stood the first place of worship built, for which Maisonneuve himself assisted to cut and draw the timbers, some of which are still in existence. The name *Bonsecours*, signifying succour, was given on account of a narrow escape of the infant colony from the Iroquois. The present building, erected in 1771 on the old foundations, was, until a few years ago, remarkable for its graceful tin roof and finely-pointed spire. The rear having since been altered in a manner entirely out of keeping with the original, which time had "painted that sober hue which makes the antiquity of churches their greatest beauty," much of the charm which made it unique has been destroyed. If it is true that it was an act of piety on the part of a devoted priest, it is another proof that zeal at times outruns correct taste.

The statue of heroic size on the new portion of the edifice, with arms uplifted as if in blessing, was the gift of a noble of Brittany. It was brought over in the

Seventeenth Century, and for two hundred years has been the patron saint of sailors, who ascribe to it miraculous powers. Its ancient pews, the crutches on the walls, and pictures which are among the first works of art brought to the country, suggest the varied scenes which have taken place around the old sanctuary since its doors were first opened for worship.

The ascent of a hundred steps reveals the daintiest and most aerial of chapels above the roof of the church. Tiny coloured windows, designed in lilies and pierced hearts, a microscopic organ, brought from France, no one knows when, and a few rows of seats are the furnishing. The altar, instead of the usual appearance, is a miniature house. Its history is as follows :—" One of the most remarkable events in the history of the Church was the sudden disappearance of the house which had been inhabited by the Holy Family at Nazareth in Galilee. This took place in 1291. As this sacred relic was about to be exposed to the danger of being destroyed by the Saracen infidels, it was miraculously raised from its foundations and transported by angels to Dalmatia, where, early in the morning, some peasants discovered on a small hill, a house without foundations, half converted into a shrine, and with a steeple like a chapel.

The next day their venerable bishop informed them that Our Lady had appeared to him and said that this house had been carried by angels from Nazareth, and was the same in which she had lived ; that the altar had been erected by the apostles, and the statue sculptured in cedar wood had been made by St. Luke. Three years afterwards it again disappeared, its luminous journey being witnessed by some Italian shepherds.

Its present position is about a mile from the Adriatic, at Loretto, just as the angels placed it six hundred years ago. Millions of pilgrims visit it from all parts of the world."

For the aerial chapel of *Bonsecours*, a fac-simile has been obtained. To render it more sacred it was placed for a period within the holy house, it touched its walls, and was blessed with holy water in the vessel from which our Lord drank. Such is the alleged history of this shrine, and the peculiar sanctity attached to it.

The extensive convent buildings of the Grey Nuns and other sisterhoods are as numerous as the churches. As the *matin* bell falls on the ear in the early morning hours, calling to prayers those who have chosen the austerities and serenities of convent life, it recalls to memory the noble band of ladies of the old aristocracy who left châteaux hoary with the traditions of a chivalrous ancestry, and dear with the memories of home, in the company of rough seamen to brave the untried perils of the ocean, a hostile country, homesickness and death, to carry spiritual and bodily healing to the savages. Their followers keep the same vigils now among the sins and sorrows of the bustling city. They glide through the streets with downcast eyes, in sombre robes, wimple and linen coif, bent on missions of church service and errands of mercy, tending the sick and suffering, and striving to win back human wrecks to a better life.

The various sisterhoods differ in degrees of austerity, the Grey Nuns being one of the least exacting. Their Foundling Hospital, it is said, had its origin in a most touching circumstance. One of the original members of the Order, Madame d'Youville, on leaving the convent gates in the middle of winter, found frozen in the ice of a little stream that then flowed near what is called Foundling street, an infant with a poignard in its heart. Since then tens of thousands of these small outcasts have found sanctuary and tender care within the cloister walls.

The daughter of Ethan Allan, the founder of Vermont, died a member of this Order.

The Carmelites are the most rigid in their requirements of service. They are small numerically and live behind high walls, and renounce forever the sight of the outside world, never leaving their cloister, and being practically dead to home and friends, sleeping, it is said, in their own coffins.

Instances have been known of a sister's assuming vows of special severity, as in the case of Jean Le Ber, of the *Congregation de Notre Dame*, a daughter of a merchant in the town, who voluntarily lived in solitary confinement from the year 1695 to 1714—nineteen years of self-immolation, when her couch was a pallet of straw, and her prayers and fastings unceasing. She denied herself everything that to us would make life desirable or even endurable—sacrificed the dearest ties of kindred, and pursued with intense fervour the self-imposed rigours of her vocation. Yet, it was not that in her nature she had no love for beauty nor craving for pleasure, for in the sacristy of the Cathedral, carefully preserved in a receptacle in which are kept the vestments of the clergy, are robes ornamented by her needle that are simply marvels of colour, design and exquisite finish. The modern robes, though gorgeous in richly-piled velvet from the looms of Lyons, heavy with gold work and embroidered with angels and figures so exquisitely wrought as to look as if painted on ivory, yet do not compare with that done by the fingers that were worn by asceticism within the walls of her cell. In the spare form, clad in thread-bare garments, there must have been crushed down a gorgeously artistic nature which found visible expression in the beautifully adorned *chasubles* of the priests and altar cloths, which are solid masses of delicate silken work on a ground of fine silver threads, the colours and lustre of which seem unimpaired by time. Six generations of priests have performed the sacrifice of the mass in these marvellously beautiful robes, the incense from the swaying censors of two hundred years have floated around them in waves of perfume. The taste and skill with which high-born ladies of that time wrought tapestries to hang on their castle walls were consecrated by her to religion, in devoting to the Church, work which was fit to adorn the royal drapings of a Zenobia.

Without the magnificence which distinguishes the cathedrals, some of the rural shrines are full of interest. The church of *Ste. Anne's,* an old building near the western end of the island, and one of the oldest sacerdotal edifices in America, has around it a halo of romance and piety since the fur-trading days, being the last church visited by the *voyageurs* and their last glimpse of civilization before facing the dangers of the pathless wilderness of the West. At its altar these rough, half-wild men knelt to pray and put themselves under the protection of their titular *Sainte Anne.*

The Trappists, though rarely seen outside the walls of their retreat, look precisely as did mediæval monks of centuries ago, with whose appearance we are familiar in pictures of Peter the Hermit and other zealots, who with their fiery eloquence sent the Armies of Christendom to fight for the Holy Sepulchre. They dress in a coarse brown gown and cowl, with a girdle of rope, and are under vows of perpetual silence. They live on frugal meals of vegetables and fruit twice a day, have the head tonsured, and feet bare in sandals. The continued fasts, severe flagellations, labours and meditations of those anchorites make the regulations governing this order exceedingly strict, and recall the times when kings and emperors, in the same monkish garb, walked barefoot to knock humbly in penance at monastery gates.

Perhaps the most unique shrine in the province is that of Mount Rigaud, on the banks of the Ottawa, not far from the spot where Dollard and his band of Christian knights lay down their lives. The mountain is regarded with much superstition by the ignorant, on account of its peculiar and unaccountable natural phenomena, whose origin has puzzled the most learned scientists to account for. The wooded mountain is crowned by what is called " The Field of Stones," or " The Devil's Garden," from a deposit of almost spherical boulders, of so far unmeasured depth, which cover its surface. Encircled by trees and verdure, this strange formation of several acres in extent is composed mainly of rock different from the mass of the mountain, which belongs to the same family as the igneous mountains of the neighbouring region. What were the causes and conditions which carried this strange material to the top of this elevation will, when they are explained, be of intense interest. It is said that the only other deposit similar, though smaller in extent, is in Switzerland. Perhaps some ancient glacier, through eons of time, gradually melted here, and slowly deposited the drift it had borne from regions far away.

A bold spur of the hill has been converted into a shrine, adorned with images, while on the bare rough sides of the lichen-covered rocks have been inscribed in large white letters the words " Penitence—Penitence." At regular intervals on the stony road approaching it are what are called the " Stations of the Cross." They are fourteen in number, being little chapels made from the uncut stones of the " Devil's Garden." The floors of these, on which the penitents kneel before pictures of the " Passion," are covered with sand and coarse gravel.

The conquest of Canada in 1759 by the English differed from that of Britain by the

Norman French in 1066, in that here the vanquished were allowed to retain their language, customs and full religious liberties, so that, after a lapse of one hundred and fifty years, the Papal service is solemnized with all the pomp and ceremonial of the Vatican, and in the courts, the Quebec Legislature and in Society is heard the euphonic French speech, and, outside of Rome, Canada is considered the chief bulwark of Papacy.

THE MASSACRE OF LACHINE.

THE conquest and settlement of all new regions are necessarily more or less written in blood, and the natural characteristics of the North American Indian have caused much of the early history of Canada to be traced in deeds of horror and agony lighted by the torture fire, with sufferings the most exquisite of which the human mind can conceive. When these were inflicted on individuals, it was sufficiently heartrending, but when a whole community fell a victim to their ferocity, as was the case in what is called " The Massacre of Lachine," the details are too horrible for even the imagination to dwell upon. Standing on the river bank, or " shooting " the rapids in the steamer, with the green shores as far as the eye can reach dotted with villages and villas, the wonderful bridges spanning the stream, and beyond, the great city with its domes and spires, it can scarcely be realized that for two days and two nights the spot was a scene of the most revolting carnage. It was an evening in the summer of 1689. In spite of a storm of wind and rain which broke over the young settlement, the fields of grain and meadows looked cheerful and thrifty. In each cabin home the father had returned from the day's toil in the harvest field and was sitting by the fireside, where the kettle sang contentedly. The mother sat spinning or knitting, and perhaps singing a lullaby, as she rocked the cradle, little recking that ere the morning dawned the hamlet would lie in ashes, and the tomahawk of the Indian be buried in her babies' hearts ; but such was the case, for after forty-eight hours of fiendish cruelty, death and desolation reigned for miles along the shores. Where the blue smoke had curled up among the trees were only the smoking ruins of hearths and homes, surrounded with sights and suggestions of different forms of death, which even the chronicler, two hundred years after, is fain to pass by in shuddering silence.

The crumbling remains of a fortified

seigniorial château, within sight of the Rapids of Lachine, a tradition asserts, was in the year 1668 the home of La Salle, who was one of the most excellent men of his day. Leaving his fair demesne, which the Sulpicians had conferred upon him, and the home which to-day is slowly falling to decay among the apple-orchards along the river side, he too followed his thirst for adventure into untrodden fields.

There is a well-founded legend that the old chimney attached thereto was built by Champlain in his trading post of logs. It is of solid masonry, and is sixty years older than the walls which surround it. The wide fireplace has a surface of fifty square feet, and is the most interesting piece of architecture in all Canada. The snowflakes of almost three hundred winters have fallen into its cavernous depths since these stones and mortar were laid. When Champlain stood by its hearth, as its first blaze, lighted by tinder and flint, roared up to the sky—William Shakespeare was still writing his sublime lines, Queen Elizabeth had lain but twelve years in her marble tomb, and the

HOME OF LA SALLE.

Château de Ramezay was not to be built for a hundred years to come. Often in the two years during which it had for La Salle the sacredness of the home fireside, its light must have fallen on his handsome young face, and flowing curls, as he laid out plans for his palisaded village, and dreamt of the golden lands towards the setting sun. He was a true patriot, and literally gave his life for the advancement of his country, being murdered in the Lower Mississippi by one of his own men while endeavouring to extend its territory.

Posterity is not true to the memory of these great pioneers, for the elements beat upon the roofless timbers, the north wind sweeps the hearth that is mouldering under the rains and sunshine of the skies they loved. In another generation all that can be said will be—here once stood the historic stones of the ancient fireside of the heroes who won the wilderness for those who have allowed this monument of their fortitude and self-sacrifice to crumble into dust.

La Salle had heard from some stray

bands of Seneca Indians, who had visited his post at Lachine, of a great river that flowed from their hunting grounds to the sea. Imagining it would open his way to find the route to the golden Ind, he sold his grant at Lachine, and in company with two priests from the Seminary at Montreal, and some Senecas as guides, started on July 6th, 1669. With visions of finding for France a clime of warmer suns and more rich in silver and gold than Canada, he pushed on. The priests on their return

La Salle

brought back nothing of any value except the first map procured of the upper lake region.

One of the most enthusiastic fellow travelers of La Salle was a Franciscan, Father Hennepin. They crossed the ocean from France together, and probably beguiled many an hour of the long voyage in relating their dreams of finding the treasures hidden in the land to which the prow of the vessel pointed.

Hennepin also penetrated to the Mississippi, reaching in his wanderings a beautiful fall foaming between its green bluffs which he named St. Anthony, on which spot now stands the " Flour City," Minneapolis, in the county of Hennepin, Minnesota. He probably heard of the other falls, five miles away, which we know as Minnehaha, and around which the sweetest of American poets has woven the witchery of Indian legend in the wooing of " Hiawatha." It seems almost incredible that where are now the largest flour mills in the world, turning out daily about 40,000 barrels, there was, scarcely fifty years ago, only the cedar strewn wigwam and smoke of the camp fire, the tread of moccasined feet and the dip of the paddles by the bark canoe.

Near by *Place d'Armes* Square may be seen a grey stone house on which is written "Here lived Sieur Du-Luth." He was a leading spirit among the young men of the town, who gathered around his fireside to listen to his thrilling tales of adventure, and of his early life when he was a *gendarme* in the King's Guard. Coming to Canada in the year 1668, he explored among the Sioux tribes of the Western plains. He was one of the first Frenchmen to approach the sources of the Mississippi. The city of Duluth in Minnesota received its name from him. A tablet on a modern building in the same locality informs the passer-by that *Cadillac*, who founded the City of Detroit about the same time as the Château de Ramezay was built, spent the last years of his wandering life on this spot.

The town of Varennes, down the river, is called from the owner of a Seigniory in the forest, le Chevalier Gauthier de la Vérandrye, a soldier and a trader, who was the first to explore the great Canadian North-West, and to discover the "Rockies." He was an undaunted and fearless traveler, establishing post after post, as far as the wild banks of the Saskatchewan and even further north, which, in giving to France, he ultimately gave to Canada.

> " Honour to those who fought the trees,
> And won the land for us."

The traditions connected with the Château de Ramezay are scarcely more interesting than those surrounding many spots in the vicinity. Incorporated in this prosaic, business part of the city are many an old gable or window, which were once part of some mediæval chapel or home of these early times. On the other side of Notre Dame street, where now stands the classic and beautiful pile called the City Hall, were to be seen in those days the church and "*Habitation*," as it was called, of the Jesuit Fathers, within whose walls lived many learned sons of Loyola, Charlevoix among others. They were burnt down in 1803, at the same time as the Château de Vaudreuil was destroyed, by one of the disastrous fires which have so frequently swept the cities of Montreal and Quebec, and in which many quaint historical structures disappeared. About a mile to the west is still standing the family residence of Daniel Hyacinthe, Marie Liénard de Beaujeu, the hero of the Monongahela, at which battle George Washington was an officer.

It was a lamentable event, the indiscriminate slaughter of three thousand men through the stupidity and incredible ob-

stancy of General Braddock, who, like Dieskau at a subsequent time, despising the counsel of those familiar with Indian methods of warfare, determinedly followed his own plans

Washington in this engagement held the rank of Adjutant-General of Virginia. " His business was to inform the French that they were building forts on English soil, and that they would do well to depart peaceably."

Beaujeu was sent at the head of a force composed of French soldiers and Indian allies to answer the Briton with the powerful argument of force of arms.

" As Braddock reached the ford over the river which was to put him on the same side as the fort, Colonel Thomas Gage crossed in advance, without opposition. Beaujeu had intended to contest the passage, but his Indians being refractory, his march was delayed. Gage with the advance was pushing on when his engineer saw a man, apparently an officer, wave his cap to his followers, who were unseen in the woods. From every vantage ground of knoll and bole, and on three sides of the column, the concealed muskets were levelled upon the English, who returned the fire. As Beaujeu fell, Dumas, who succeeded him, thought that the steady front of the redskins was going to carry the day, until he saw his Canadians fly, followed by the Indians, after Gage had wheeled his cannon on the woods. A little time, however, changed all this. The Indians rallied and poured their bullets into the massed and very soon confused British troops. Braddock, when he spurred forward, found everybody demoralized except the Virginians, who were firing from the tree trunks, as the enemy did. The British General was shocked at such an unmilitary habit, and ordered them back into line. No one under such orders could find cover, and every puff from a concealed Indian was followed by a soldier's fall. No exertion of Braddock, nor of Washington, nor of any one prevailed. The General had four horses shot under him and Washington had two. Still the hillsides and the depths of the wood were spotted by puffs of smoke, and the slaughter-pen was in a turmoil—scarce one Englishman in three escaped bullets. The commander then gave the sign to retreat, and was endeavouring to restore order when a ball struck him from his horse. The British Army had become bewildered fugitives, and a guard could hardly be kept for the wounded General, as he was borne along on a horse as a litter.

The sinking Braddock at last died and was buried in the road, that the tramp of the surging mass of men might obliterate his grave. His remains are said to have been discovered in 1823 by some workmen engaged in constructing the National road, at a spot pointed out by an old man who had been in the ranks in 1755. He claimed to have seen Braddock buried, and to have fired the bullet that killed him. It was impossible to identify the remains almost seventy years after their interment, but with them were found bits of military trappings, so his tale may have been correct. In the year 1841, near to the spot, was discovered a large quantity of shot and shell left by the retreating army.

Adjoining the grounds of the Château de Ramezay was the mansion of General Ralph Burton, who fought close to Wolfe in the siege of Quebec, to whom his dying words were spoken, and who carried out his last command, which decided the day. As Wolfe lay half unconscious, the riot of the battle growing dull on his failing senses, they were roused by the cry, "They run!" He opened his glazed eyes and asked, "Who run?" and the reply was, "The French!" With a supreme effort he turned to Burton, and ordered him, saying, "Command Webb to march down to the St. Charles and cut off the retreat at the bridge"; and then amid the crash and carnage of war, he murmured, "Now I thank God, and die contented," and instantly expired.

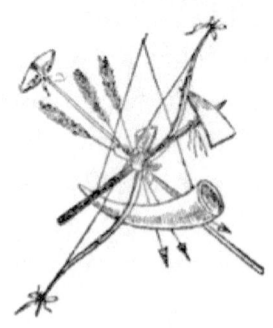

THE CHATEAU DE VAUDREUIL.

A SHORT distance to the south-west is the spot on which stood the Château and famous gardens of the Marquis de Vaudreuil, the last French Governor of Canada. Imagination can forget the miles of docks and warehouses, the electricity and commerce with which we are entering the twentieth century, and fancy it sees again the old vice-regal palace, a miniature in Canadian forests of the gay court at the Tuilleries, with its bewitchment of lace, silk and velvet, powdered wigs and the exaggerated politeness and exquisite bows of *la grande dame* and *le chevalier* of the time.

Let us step back to the winter of 1758 and '59. The mountain is snow-capped and the St. Lawrence is frozen several feet thick, making good roads for the shaggy Canadian pony and *cariole*, or heavy *traineau* with wooden runners. In the early winter's evening, lights gleam through the small windows of the earthen citadel which guards the *Porte St. Martin*, and the clash of arms or halberds, and the pacing of the sentries' footsteps, are heard at every closed gate of the little walled town. Patches of warm light from candle and hearth checker the snow which lies glistening on the sidewalks, for there are no street lamps on the St. Paul, St. Mary or Notre Dame streets of these old days.

Under the night sky, the storehouses look like gloomy prisons, but cheerful groups talk and laugh, as the beaux and belles bend their steps along the narrow streets to the Governor's salon. As the guests of the Marquis de Vaudreuil assemble, the brilliance of their costumes is heightened in effect by the gorgeous livery of the attendants and the blue and white of the soldiers' regimentals. Groups around the spindle-legged card tables exchange *bon-mots* and play, while others dance and promenade on the polished floors until the morning light breaks over the river.

The gaiety and frivolity, feasting and gossip are in strange contrast to the grey gown of the Jesuit priest hurrying from the monastery opposite, to shrive some sinner, or to administer "Extreme Unction" to some dying saint. Within the convent walls pious sisters, followers of Mademoiselle Mance and Madame d'Youville, tend the sick and unfortunate, whom the tide of life has cast upon this far away shore. From the taverns on the corners and on the river front comes

the sound of mirth and merriment, as with the cup of good Gascon wine are passed around tales of the high seas or of times gone by in the old-world towns of Brittany.

On the altars of the chapels lights burn dimly in a silence unbroken, save by the murmuring of prayers and telling of beads by suppliants driven hither by sin, sorrow or homesickness.

A narrow little street, named St. Amable, running west from the Governor's mansion, has been subjected to so little change since those days of long ago that the passer-by on its two feet of sidewalk sees it just as it was when its vaulted warehouses held the cargoes of the weather-beaten sailing craft that anchored at the shore below. Where now the French *habitant* sits chattering with his *confrères* and smoking his pipe filled with home-grown *tabac* were once the shady walks and stiff parterres of the ancient garden. Here, under the summer moons, were doubtless stolen meetings as sweet, vows as insincere, and intrigues as

RUE ST. AMABLE.

COPYRIGHT.

foolish as those in the exquisite bowers of *Le Petit Trianon* at Versailles. On its paths have fallen the martial tread of " de Lévis, de Beaujeu, and many a brave soldier and dainty courtier, official guests at the Governor's Château." Among them was one who eclipsed all others in sad interest, the courtly young commander, Louis Joseph Saint Veran de Montcalm. Any spot associated with this ill-fated general is of immortal memory. After his skillful manœuvering at the battle of Carillon, his march to Montreal was a triumph. At the close of this engagement, as, accompanied by de Lévis and his staff, he rode along the ranks, thanking his troops, who idolized him, in the name of their king, for their glorious display of French valour in a field where thirty-six hundred men had for six hours withstood fifteen thousand, he was in every particular a worthy and capable general. He spoke of his own share in the glory of the day with simplicity and modesty, writing the next day to Vaudreuil :—

"The only credit I can claim as accruing to me is the glory of commanding troops so valorous."

On one occasion, the capture of Oswego, which is described as the most brilliant military exploit then known in Canadian history, he with his own hand snatched the colours from a British officer and sent the trophy to Quebec, to adorn the walls of the Cathedral of that city; as many a time before had been done for old-world Minsters by knights on the battlefields of Europe, whose empty armour now hangs in the baronial halls of England.

Montcalm had been summoned to Montreal to confer with the Governor on the further conduct of the war, and, as he marched forth to take command of the Citadel of Quebec, all hearts centred on him, saying, "Save for France her fair dominion in the West;" but the gallant soldier, in his endeavour to do so, met his tragic and untimely end.

Entrenched behind the ramparts of Quebec, he prepared for the great struggle which was to decide the fortunes of the then two foremost powers of Europe. He and de Lévis, although a considerable distance from each other, had seventeen thousand men under their command, with a splendid line of fortifications running from Montmorenci to the St. Charles, supplementing the granite defences of the Citadel. Montcalm being in doubt for some time at what point to look for attack from the enemy, sent orders along the whole line for his troops to

Louis Joseph Marquis de Montcalm

be in perfect readiness everywhere. He was several years older than Wolfe, and was an old campaigner, having served his king with honour and distinction in Germany, Italy and Bohemia.

THE BATTLE OF THE PLAINS.

IT was the evening of the 12th of Sept., 1759. The French troops were on the alert,—the British ready. The evening was calm and fine and the occasion full of solemnity as Wolfe embarked in a boat to visit some of his posts. As the oars dipped softly in the stream, and the quiet dusk of the autumn twilight hid the grim signs of war and brought out the peaceful beauty of the scene, he thought of the morrow—that where

" Now fades the glimmering landscape on the sight,
 And all the air a solemn stillness holds,"

would be rent by the roar of cannon, the flash of bloody steel and the cries of the wounded and dying.

Feeling perhaps a shrinking from the great crisis which the dawn would bring, he repeated to the officers and midshipmen within hearing a number of the verses from the most finished poem in the English language, Grey's " Elegy in a

Country Churchyard," and which had appeared a short time before. Probably the lines on which he lingered longest were :—

> " The boast of heraldry, the pomp of power,
>   And all that beauty, all that wealth e'er gave,
> Await alike the inevitable hour;
>   The paths of glory lead but to the grave."

The last line was, alas ! prophetic in his own case, and he may have had some premonition of it, for turning to his listeners, who were to share with him victory or defeat, he said with a wistful pathos in his young voice, " I would prefer being the author of that poem to the glory of beating the French to-morrow."

He did not dream that for what that morrow would bring, his name, with that of the poet he loved, would be carven among those of England's great men in Westminster Abbey—

> " Where thro' the long-drawn aisle and fretted vault
>   The pealing anthem swells the note of praise."

Landing in a ravine (Wolfe's Cove), which he had located by the use of a glass—with the strategic venture at which all the world has since wondered—in the dark hours of the same night, he, at the head of the famous Fraser Highlanders, placed his force on the Plains of Abraham, each man knowing it was victory or death, as there was no possibility of retreat.

The intelligence of the landing of the British troops was first brought to the Governor-General, the Marquis de Vaudreuil, and he had the task of communicating the unwelcome news to Montcalm, who had hurried from his quarters on the ramparts to ascertain what was the meaning of the firing above the town.

On learning the situation, he bitterly exclaimed :—

"They have at least got to the weak side of this miserable garrison, and, therefore, we must endeavour to crush them by our numbers before 12 o'clock."

Montcalm, with more courage than discretion, without waiting for de Lévis, who was twenty-eight miles away,—the victim of an inexorable destiny, unsupported led forth his men, and saw, not without surprise, the whole British Army ranged in battle array. Without giving his men time to recover breath after the fatigue of their laborious and hurried march, he went into action, trusting to the well-tested courage of his troops.

Wolfe led the charge at the head of the Louisburg Grenadiers, and when the Highlanders, throwing away their muskets, rushed on with their broad swords

like a tempest of steel, the hapless blue coats, though lacking in neither prowess nor patriotism, fled in all directions. The two young leaders fell almost simultaneously.

When Wolfe received his death wound, he was in a conspicuous spot near the Redoubt, and was thence borne to the rear. He had calmly prepared for this contingency. He had made his will, of which he appointed Sir Guy Carleton the executor, and for whom he had early formed a close friendship, generally speaking of him as "My friend Carleton," and to whom he bequeathed his books and papers. His plate he willed to Saunders, and to another friend he entrusted the miniature of his betrothed with the charge of returning it to her in the event of his fall. That was probably the most trying moment of those hours so fraught with tragedy—a moment like those on the eve of Waterloo, when there were

"Partings that crush the life from out young hearts."

It was not in his martial cloak nor in

his country's flag that he was carried dead off the field, but in the tartan "plaidie" of an old Highland man, named McLeod, which was tenderly wrapped around him, wet with tears from eyes to which tears had long been strangers.

As he fell, his principal care was for the effect it would have upon his troops, who, down to the humblest in his command, had caught his spirit, and who felt that "they must fulfil the trust reposed in them, or die in the ranks."

Leaning against the shoulder of the officer who caught him when falling, he implored him to support him, saying, "Do not let my brave soldiers see me drop, the day is ours, keep it!" A death attended with circumstances more pathetic or incidents more picturesque the annals of war do not record.

"The capture of Quebec was an achievement of so formidable a character, so distinguished by chivalrous enterprise, and so fraught with singular adventure, that the interest attending it still remains undimmed and its glorious recollections unfaded."

The virtues and heroism of the youthful leader of the campaign and the bravery of his troops, whose toast was "The British flag on every fort, post and garrison in America," are themes of just pride to the lover of his country. "Young in years but mature in experience, Wolfe possessed all the liberal virtues in addition to an enthusiastic knowledge of the military art with a sublimity of genius, always the distinguishing mark of minds above the ordinary level of mankind. His celebrated letter to Mr. Pitt is still considered unsurpassed in military composition."

As Montcalm was carried off the field he enquired if his wound was mortal; on being answered in the affirmative, with a mental anguish keener than the intense physical pain he was suffering, he said, "So much the better, I shall not live to see the surrender of Quebec." Few scenes are more full of sadness than his march from his last battle-field, as supported by two grenadiers, and passing through the St. Louis Gate on his black charger, he courteously greeted the weeping women who lined his path, telling them not to weep for him ; but it could not be but a day of tears for the daughters of Quebec as groans of mortal agony came to their ears through the smoke and dust of retreat.

A few hours afterward, on being visited by M. de Ramezay, who commanded the garrison, with the title of Lieutenant *du Roy*, and another officer, Montcalm addressed them saying, " Gentlemen, I commend to your keeping the honour of France,—for myself. I shall pass the night with God, and prepare myself for death."

On M. de Ramezay's pressing to receive commands respecting the defence of Quebec, he exclaimed with emotion :—" I will neither give orders nor interfere further. I have business that must be attended to of greater moment than your ruined garrison and this wretched country. My time is very short, so pray leave me ; I wish you all comfort, and to be happily extricated from your present difficulties."

Before expiring, he paid a noble tribute to his late foes, when he said :—

"Since it was my misfortune to be discomfited and mortally wounded, it is a great consolation to me to be vanquished by so brave and generous an enemy. If I could survive this wound, I would engage to beat three times the number of such forces as I commanded this morning with a third of such troops as were opposed to me."

Almost his last conscious act was to write a letter praying the English victors to show clemency to the French prisoners.

It is said that a fissure ploughed by a cannon ball within the walls of the Ursuline Convent furnished him a fitting soldier's grave.

One of the sisterhood, an eye-witness of the event, described the burial in the following touching and graphic words:—

"At length it was September, with its lustrous skies and pleasant harvest scenes. The city was destroyed, but it was not taken. Would not the early autumn, so quickly followed by winter, force the enemy to withdraw their fleet? For several days the troops which had been so long idle were moving in various directions above and below Quebec, but they were watched and every point guarded, but no one dreamed of the daring project the intrepid Wolfe was meditating. The silence of the night told no tale of the stealthy march of five thousand soldiers. The echoes of the high cliff only brought to the listening boatmen the necessary password. No rock of the shelving precipice gave way under the cat-like tread of the Highlanders accustomed to the crags of their native hills, but the morning light glittered on serried rows of British bayonets, and in an hour the battle of the Plains changed the destinies of New France. The remnant of the French army, after turning many times on their pursuers, completely disappeared. Their tents were still standing on the Plains of Beauport, but their batteries were silent and trenches empty—their guns still pointed, but were mute.

"At nine o'clock in the evening a funeral *cortège* issuing from the castle, wound its way through the dark and obstructed streets to the little church of the Ursulines.

The measured foot steps of the military escort kept time with the heavy tread of the bearers, as the officers of the garrison followed the lifeless remains of their illustrious commander-in-chief to their last resting place. No martial pomp was displayed around that humble bier and rough wooden box, which were all the ruined city could afford the body of her defender ; but no burial rite could be more solemn than that hurried evening service performed by torchlight under the war-scarred roof of the Convent, as with tears and sighs were chanted the words 'Libera me Domine.' "

Some years ago an Englishman, Lord Aylmer, caused to be placed within the convent enclosure a tablet with the words carved in marble :—

Honneur
à
Montcalm.
Le Destin en lui dérobant
La Victoire,
L'a récompensé par
Une Mort Glorieuse.

Or, Honor to Montcalm. Fate denied him victory, but rewarded him with a glorious death. Byron expresses a similar sentiment when he said :—

"They never fail who die in a good cause."

On the spot where Wolfe fell has been raised a simple shaft on which is written :—

"Here Wolfe died victorious,
Sept. 13th, 1759,
In the thirty-fourth year of his age."

The stone which formed his death couch is preserved in its original position, but sunk beneath the ground to protect it from the ravages of the relic hunter. The column is supported on a pedestal of rocks formed of boulders from the scene of the battle, conspicuous among which may be seen the actual rock upon which Wolfe was supported when he breathed his last. The stones of the monument are strongly cemented together, embedded in the solid foundation of rock, and will be as enduring as the fame of him whose name it bears.

The well near by, from which the water

THE BATTLE OF THE PLAINS. 115

was brought to allay his thirst, was filled up and obliterated some years ago, much to the regret of those who venerated the immortal incident connected with it, and which placed it among the historic shrines of the world.

Chas. Saunders

Associated with Wolfe, and a sharer in the glory of the capture of Quebec, was Charles Saunders, commander of the squadron. By bombarding the town, he kept the enemy in a state of constant and anxious alarm, at the same time showing wonderful skill in cleverly protecting his fleet from disaster; even when threatened by fire-ships sent to destroy it, which were grappled by the British sailors and run aground.

Among those who rendered signal service to Admiral Saunders when he neared Quebec was the famous navigator, Captain Cook. He was the pilot who conducted the boats to the attack at Montmorency on July 31st, 1759, and managed the disembarkment at the Heights of Abraham.

The great mariner, while engaged in his celebrated voyages of discovery, was murdered by South Sea Islanders at Owhyhee on the 14th of Feby., 1779. He had been sent by the British Government to find if the discovery of the North-West passage, which seemed impossible by the Atlantic, were feasible by the Pacific Ocean; for which purpose he had to round the southern part of the entire American Continent. He was on the point of abandoning the project and returning home when he met his terrible death, "leaving a name unsurpassed for gallantry by any sea-faring man of his time."

In the month of October Saunders' fleet dropped silently down the river. On one of the ships was the embalmed body of James Wolfe, returning to the land he had served so well, but where alas! he would never hear the acclamations with which his fellow countrymen, from the palace to the cabin, would lay the laurel wreath upon his tomb,—the paths of glory had truly led but to the grave!

Saunders on his return was appointed Lieutenant-General of Marine, and on taking his seat as a member of the House of Commons received the thanks of the Speaker. He became Knight Commander of the Bath, and on his death was buried in Westminster Abbey near to the Monument of Wolfe.

Of the regiments to whom England owes the Conquest of Canada, the Scotch claim the greatest share of glory. "Hardy sons of mountain and heather, they were in fact the flower of the army, the boldest in attack, the fiercest at close quarters, the last to retreat at command, and always the bravest of the brave in the forefront of England's battles."

The kilted "laddies" from beyond the Grampians, in their "*braw*" plumed bonnets, with their war-pipes lilting above the loudest din of war, have met some of the fiercest onslaughts singing and stepping to the blood-stirring strains of "Scots wha ha'e wi' Wallace bled."

An eye-witness of their march out of Brussels on that beautiful June morning in 1815, the dawn of Waterloo, says:

"One could not but admire their fine appearance, their steady military demeanour, with their pipes playing before them, and the beams of the rising sun shining on their glittering arms." Many of the young officers were in the silk stockings and dancing pumps which they wore the night before to the Duchess of Richmond's ball, when they laughed:—

"On with the dance, let joy be unconfined,
 No sleep till morn when youth and beauty meet,
 To chase the glowing hours with flying feet."

With swords waving, the pibroch screaming and the " stirring memories of a thousand years," they rushed into the stupendous conflict leading the "*Forty-twa*" into the field, which the setting of the same sun saw drenched through with blood, but marked by deeds which covered with glory many a thatched ingle-nook on highland hills and in lowland valleys.

After the Conquest of Canada, the Fraser Highlanders with the remains of the 42nd were offered grants of land if they chose to remain as settlers, a privilege which many of them accepted. Sixteen years afterward, when a foreign invasion threatened Canada, they loyally left the plough in the furrow and again sprang to arms, to protect their altars and firesides.

Among the blue Laurentian hills of the lower St. Lawrence, around their simple hearths, their descendants live the placid life of the Canadian *habitant*. They bear the old historic names of their Gaelic forefathers,—Fraser, Cameron, Blackburn, MacDonald, etc.—but in nothing else could it be thought that in their veins runs the blood of those who fought at Colloden and Bannockburn. They are as purely French in their religion, language and customs, as those whose sires sailed from Breton and Norman ports.

The Commandant of Quebec at the time of its fall was the son of Claude de Ramezay, the builder of the Château of that name. After the disastrous battle, Vaudreuil, Governor of Montreal, sent him urgent charges to do his utmost to hold out until reinforcements, which were on a forced march from Montreal and elsewhere, should arrive to his succour; but, the besieged being in the greatest extreme of fright and starvation, his force refused to fight. His conduct has been much criticized, but one annalist asserts that he was "not the man to shrink from danger or death had there been anything but foolhardiness in the risk, as he belonged to the good old fighting stock of North Britain,"—the race which produced a Wallace and a Bruce. He, however, signed the articles of capitulation, as recommended by the Council of War summoned, and the British marched in through the iron-spiked gates,—when, had he held out only twenty-four hours longer, Canada might have been saved for France, as the British could not for any length of time have maintained their position on the Plains of Abraham. Returning to France, where he was related to several families of the Noblesse, who held that "war was the only worthy calling, and prized honour more than life," he received so cool a reception at Court that his proud spirit, being unable to brook the humiliation, he applied for a passport allowing him to return to Canada, but subsequently he abandoned the idea of returning to his native land. Had he carried out his intention, he might have seen French, English and American flags successively wave over the red roof of the Château of his boyhood.

To complete the conquest, Montreal was attacked at three different points by Generals Amherst, Murray and Haldimand. Arriving within a few hours of each other, they camped outside of the old walls of the town. Vaudreuil and de Lévis tried to oppose them, but with Quebec lost, and the only defences a rude citadel and weak walls built to resist Indian attack and useless in civilized warfare, they were compelled to surrender. A small stone cottage, until quite recently standing in a private garden on the mountain side, was used as Amherst's headquarters, and in which the articles of capitulation were signed between the victorious and vanquished generals.

Among those who entered the town with Amherst was Israel Putnam, a man who had been brought into Montreal a year before a prisoner by the French. He had great physical strength and decision of character, and was absolutely incapable of fear. On the breaking out of the Revolutionary War, he entered with zeal into the cause of the colonists, and lead them in the battle of Bunker Hill. True to his convictions, he refused the large sums of money offered him by the British for his services. By the American troops he was lovingly called "Old Put."

On his tombstone was inscribed:—" He dared to lead where any dared to follow."

As the British entered the city by the old Recollet Monastery gate, the French retired to *la Citadelle,* a strong wood block house at the other end of the town. General Haldimand was the First Englishman to enter within the walls, remains of which are still frequently dug up in excavating. The oldest Ensign in Amherst's army received the French colours, and it is said the keys of the city were given over by a woman, but it is recorded with certainty that the fallen foes were treated with the greatest consideration and respect, not even the Indian allies being permitted to commit a single act of violence. "Amherst commanded the principal division, including the 'Black Watch,' or gallant 42nd, which has been renowned in military story wherever the British flag has been borne to victory for more than a hundred and forty years." At Waterloo, Corunna, Alma and Lucknow, in Afghan defiles and Egyptian deserts, they were always in the thickest of the fight.

It is said, Pitt, wanting a safe and sure officer to command them, chose what he called a stubborn Colonel, who had shown his mettle in Germany, and made him Major-General Amherst.

CANADA UNDER ENGLISH RULE.

GENERAL James Murray, the son of Lord Elibank, was appointed the first British Governor of Canada. Previous to the fall of Montreal, de Lévis, refusing to consider the cause of France lost on the St. Lawrence, valiantly resolved on an attack on General Murray at Quebec. The news of his advance was conveyed to Murray by a "half-frozen *cannonier*, whom the British troops carried up Mountain Hill in a sailor's hammock."—April 26th, 1760. Hearing of this unfortunate circumstance, which gave up to the enemy his intention of taking him unawares, de Lévis hurriedly led his men under the walls of the city, where Murray, promptly coming out to meet him, the battle of "Ste. Foye" took place, when the French this time saw their efforts crowned with success, the British having to find a shelter within the walls of the old Citadel. The French leader was too weak to operate a regular siege, so remained camped on the battle-field, awaiting the reinforcements expected.

de Levis

One bright sunny morning it was heralded on all sides that a fleet had been signalled, and the joy of the French troops knew no bounds; but, alas! for them it was found out but too soon that the ships were under England's flag. Instead of de Lévis receiving the assistance he required, it came to the already victorious Briton. It but remained, therefore, for him to retire in haste to Montreal, where, being soon followed up by the enemy and surrounded on all sides, he had to submit to the dictates of fate, as already stated.

He affixed his name to the Articles of Capitulation, with, it is said, the document placed against a tree at the head of St. Helen's Island.

De Lévis, although blamed for his unsoldierlike act in the destruction of his regimental colours, was, nevertheless, a fine specimen of the long line of chivalrous nobles, whose names and deeds emblazon French chronicles of field and foray since the days when Charlemagne wore his iron crown. Deeply chagrined at the refusal of the British to allow the garrison to march out with the honours of war, although high-spirited to a fault, he humbled himself to pray in writing for the reversal of the order. It may have been in the salon of the Château that the representatives of the two knights stood face to face as suppliant and arbiter. Their fathers may have crossed swords at Crécy, when the Plantagenet Prince bore off the feathered crest which was to be the insignia of all future first-born sons of English kings, or they may have tilted with lance and pennon on the Field of the Cloth of Gold ; but here de Lévis, with his petition sternly denied, was forced to retire in anger, filled with humiliation at the failure of his intercession.

It may be imagined with what conflicting emotions he entered the following words in his journal :—

"The British sent a detachment to *Place d'Armes* with artillery, whither our battalions marched one after another, to lay down their arms, and the enemy took possession of the posts and watches of the city." As they filed past the Château, which was on their line of march, many a heavy heart beat beneath the blue coats, and when a few days later they embarked with their chief for France, even valour need not have been ashamed if tears dimmed the sight of the English colours flying from their flag staffs, and the fair land fading from their sight forever.

The Château de Vaudreuil was then dismantled of its treasures of fine china and specimens of the arts revived in what is known as the *Renaissance*, when everything that was exquisite in painting, sculpture, working in metals, and art in all its forms had received such an impetus from the Italian artists whom Louis the Fourteenth gathered around his court, as well as from the influence of Madame de Pompadour, whose taste, unhappily, far exceeded her morals. It was purchased by Chartier de Lotbinière, and it is pleasant to chronicle that a few years ago his direct descendant, M. de Léry Macdonald, while visiting France, had the honour of meeting la Comtesse de Clairemont-Tonnerre, the last living representative of the De Vaudreuil family, who graciously presented to him the

"*Croix St. Louis,*" which had been bestowed upon the first Vaudreuil who held an official position in Canada, which relic is now to be seen in the Château de Ramezay.

The old fortifications of Ville Marie were planned by a de Léry; he, and the military engineer who traced out his campaigns with Bonaparte, and whom he called the "*Immortel Général,*" were members of this family, in the possession of which are priceless old tapestries, which were gifts from royalty as rewards of diplomatic or personal services.

About a year after the evacuation of Quebec, Murray was sitting in the chilliness of an October evening by the chimney meditating. As he gazed at the glowing fire of maple logs, he may have fancied that he saw again the face of his dead commander, and may have thought of that desperate charge outside the gates—of the shouts of victory and cries of defeat—where then the only sound to be heard was the wind rustling the withered grass that had been dyed red in the blood of so many gallant young hearts. The soldier's face may have softened as he thought of the old hearthstone among the heather hills, where tales of the Border and the traditions of his clan had fired his young soul for the glory of conquest.

He was suddenly aroused from his dream by the announcement that two warlike frigates were sailing below the cliffs. He hurried to the bastion, which commanded the spot, to survey what might portend fresh struggles and more bloodshed. But soon a standard was run up to the masthead, unfolding to the breeze the flag of England. Immediately from the ramparts, where so recently had proudly floated the flag of France, an answering signal was shown, and, as the guns roared out a salute to the British colours, it was also a farewell honour to the old *Régime*, which has passed away forever from Canadian shores.

Of Murray, the first British Governor of Canada, it has been said that, in the long roll of unblemished good service, in the record of his honourable fidelity to his trust and duty, no passage of his life stands out in brighter colours than this period, during which he turned a deaf ear to intolerance and the spirit of persecution, and strove to show the new subjects of the Crown how truly beneficent, just and good, with all its errors, the rule of Great Britain had ever proved to be.

With the Treaty of Paris in 1763 King George III. abolished the French laws, substituting for them the English Code in the newly won Dominion; later on, however, by the "Quebec Act," they were restored to the Canadians.

The members of the *Noblesse*, whose ties compelled their remaining in Canada, sent to London to offer fealty to King George, and thus further their personal interests.

When the Chevalier de Léry and his wife, the beautiful Louise de Brouages, one of the most lovely women of her day, were presented at the Court of St. James, the young Sovereign was so struck with her beauty that he gallantly exclaimed :—

"If all Canadian ladies resemble her, we have indeed made a conquest."

A French writer of the time says :—

"How can we sufficiently deplore the loss of Canada, with all its present value and with all its future hope—a possession of which all the difficulties were already overcome, and of which the consequent advantages were secure and within reach ! That loss might have been guarded against—yes, that land consecrated by the blood of a Montcalm, a Jumonville, and so many brave Frenchmen who shared their dangers, and were united with them in fate—that country honoured with the name of New France—that country where we may yet trace her children enjoying the manners and customs of their forefathers—that country might yet have existed under its rightful princes, if the Cabinet of Versailles had known the true position it held—had erected there a new throne and had placed upon it a Prince of the Royal Family—it would have ruled to-day over that vast region, and preserved the treasures vainly spent in its defence."

After the conquest the Château de Ramezay was saved from being a mere fur-trading post by becoming the city residence of the Baron de Longueuil, a Canadian feudal lord, the towers, embattlements and chapel of whose castle were visible on the south side of the river. The founder of this house, which to-day holds the only hereditary feudal barony of Canada, was Charles LeMoyne, who came to Canada in 1642 with Maisonneuve. This man was the son of an innkeeper at Dieppe (France), who it is alleged was descended from a younger branch of the old Norman family of LeMoyne, the head of the house being the Marquis de Longueuil.

Fourteen years after his arrival in Canada, LeMoyne received the Seigniory of Longueuil, he having in the meantime amassed a considerable fortune in the fur trade.

The eldest son, who was named after

his father, was born in 1656, and in recognition of his services at a siege of Quebec, and against the Iroquois, he was made a Baron of France in 1700 by Louis 14th. The old deed of nobility is to this day in an almost perfect condition.

An original sketch of the Château de Longueuil, taken after a fire which partially destroyed it in 1792, is still in possession of the family. The Château, or in reality the Castle, was built by the first Baron in 1699, and for nearly a hundred years sheltered the family of LeMoyne.

It stood partly on the ground now occupied by the front of the present parish church of Longueuil, and partly across the highway, at a corner of the Chambly road. The north-west tower was located as late as 1835, but was covered with earth by the excavation for the new church. The Château, comprising the chapel, was 210 by 170 feet, and was constructed in the strongest possible manner of stones which were gathered by the river bank. The building was two storeys in height all around, and was flanked by four towers with conical tops. There were high gables over the building, and in the centre a court. On the river-side front it was loop-holed for defence, and it was here that the retainers came in time of trouble. On the west side was the chapel, which was large and extensive.

After the fire it was never again occupied, and later on the stone work went to help make the present roadway, as had been the fate of many an Italian palace and temple of Greece. The family gave the land where the present church stands, and they also built the first church, with vaults below. This was done on condition that the family should all be buried there, and so far this has been carried out. The barony was once very extensive, taking in a territory of about one hundred and fifty square miles, including St. Helen's Island, upon which may still be recognized the ruins of the residence which stood on the eastern side of it, Capt. Grant and his wife, Madame de Baronne de Longueuil, having lived there for some time.

Fort Senneville, an interesting ruin, at the western end of Montreal Island, and which was destroyed by Benedict Arnold at the invasion of Canada, during the American Revolution, was erected by the Le Ber family, which was closely allied to that of LeMoyne, and was enobled at the same time as the latter. The fort was intended for a fortified fur-trading post.

In 1880 the seventh Baron claimed royal recognition from the English Crown of his title to the old French Barony, which Queen Victoria was graciously pleased to recognize. The de Longueuil family was always generously treated by royalty, and on the Richelieu river are several Seigniories which have been granted to members of it. On the same side of the river St. Lawrence, but a considerable distance inland, is the pretty town of Iberville. It is named after LeMoyne d'Iberville, a member of this family, who, with his seven brothers, took their several names from their seigniories, and were all distinguished for daring and ambition in all the perilous adventures of New France in their day.

Le Moyne D'Iberville

In the Indian village of Caughnawaga, situated near the Lachine Rapids, is the half-ruined Curial House, if it may be so called, of the early historian, the Jesuit Charlevoix. Like all French travellers of that period, he had his visions of reaching the Pacific coast, which, although never realized, yet he was a celebrated explorer and an accurate and painstaking writer. His "*Histoire Générale de la Nouvelle France*" is a valuable and authentic history of the period it covers, and is looked upon as one of the most reliable authorities to-day.

In this thrifty hamlet, clustering around the church, under whose steeple worship the remnants of the once fierce and dreaded Iroquis, are the last of their race. They are adroit in the use of the canoe, and for many years have acted as pilots for the St. Lawrence steamers in the perilous navigation of the Rapids. The squaws are skilful in the bead work so dear to the savage heart, and form picturesque groups in blankets and moccasins exposing their wares for sale in the railway stations.

About ten years after the British occupation, the Château de Ramezay fell again into government hands, being selected as the official residence. One of those who frequently crossed its threshhold at this period was General Thomas Gage, second in command under Sir Jeffrey Amherst.

He was the first British Governor of Montreal, and the last of Massachusetts, and was remarkable for his doughty deeds during the American Revolution. And then in these rooms, where so often had sparkled French wit and wine, highborn English dames held sway, with the grand manners and stately dances of Queen Charlotte's Drawing Rooms at Windsor Castle. These doors were none too large for the extended skirts and towering head-dresses, some of which had satin cushions large enough to have had the family coat of arms painted on them, and yet had room to spare. The ladies naturally followed the fashions set by the Queen, who was exceedingly fond of display in dress, and had an oriental love for gems. A description of one of her toilettes has come down to us, which was almost barbaric in its profusion of ornaments. At the first

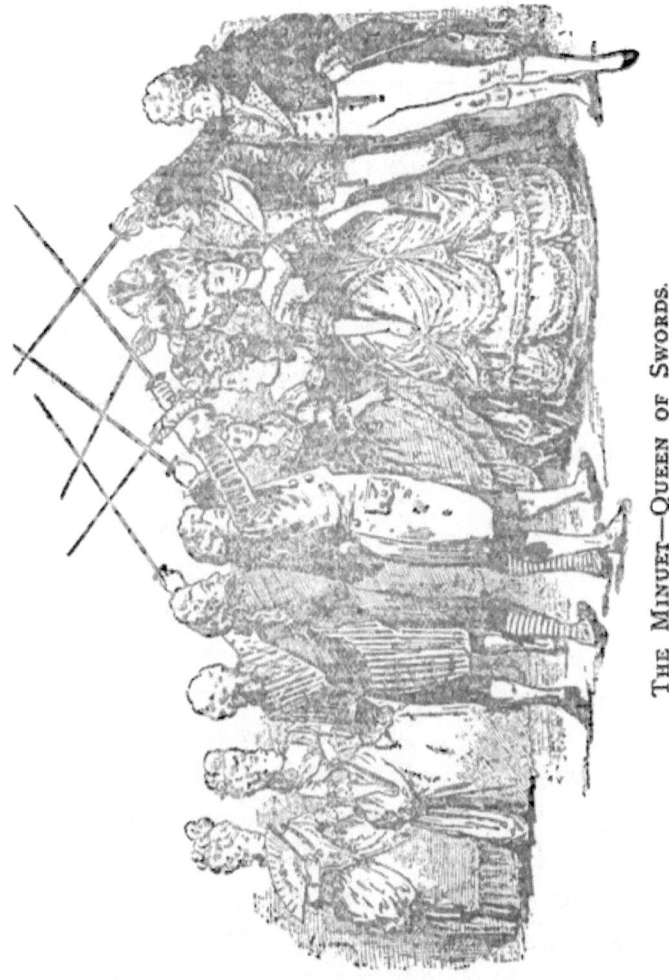

The Minuet—Queen of Swords.

Drawing Room held after King George's recovery from a dangerous illness, she "fairly glittered in a blaze of diamonds. Around her neck was a double row of these gems, to which was suspended a medallion. Across her shoulders were festooned three rows of costly pearls, and the portrait of the King was hung upon the back of her skirt from five rows of brilliants, producing a gorgeous effect. The tippet was of fine lace, fastened with the letter G. in diamonds of immense size and value, and in Her Majesty's hair was —' God save the King,' in letters formed of the same costly gems."

Under her sovereignty the guttural Anglo-Saxon tongue was heard in the homes and on the streets mingling with the mellifluent French, and the liturgy of Westminster Abbey was solemnized side by side with the ritual of St. Peter's in the hush of Sabbaths, after the din and clamour of war had ceased, and quiet once more reigned in the grey old town.

As memorials of those days of strife, carnage and conquest, some Canadian names have taken root in British soil. Gen. James Murray chose the name of Beauport for his country seat, and that of the Earls of Amherst, among the hop gardens and rose hedges of Kent, bears the name of Montreal, Amherst having been created Baron of Montreal.

AMERICAN INVASION.

IN the year 1775, when the thirteen American Colonies had risen in arms against the Motherland, it was to be expected that they would desire to have the assistance of those north of the forty-ninth parallel. Being so recently laid under British allegiance, it was supposed there would be much sympathy for the young cause in the Canadian Colonies. But, whether the treaty which had been made had been considered gracious in its terms, or that the horrible memories of war had not had time to die away, or from a combination of causes, the French-English provinces refused to take up the Colonial grievances. To compel them to do this, an expedition, consisting of Col. Ethan Allen and his " Green Mountain Boys," was detached against Montreal. Arriving on the opposite bank of the river, just below the town, with about one hundred and fifty men, he crossed over from Longueuil and reached the eastern suburbs at about ten o'clock p.m., when he proceeded to billet his men in private houses. That was before the days of telephones, so it was some time before the news reached the city and the gates were closed. The rash project of so small a force attempting to beleaguer a walled town of fourteen thousand inhabitants could have but one outcome, and it resulted in the capture of Ethan Allen. He was brought in through the Quebec Gate, or *Porte St. Martin*, sent to England and lodged in Pendennis Castle, where he could hear the moan of the wide sea that separated him from the land he loved and longed to fight for.

But the expedition was not abandoned on account of this repulse, for soon General Montgomery appeared. Rattray describes Montgomery as a brave officer of generous and exemplary character. He was an Irishman, a lieutenant in the 17th Foot, but resigned his commission in the year 1772, owing, it is said, to some grievance connected with promotion; when he settled and married in the State of New York.

Crossing the Canadian lines he captured Forts St. Jean and Chambly, the latter a stone fortress on the site of a post built by Tracey's men, and thus he became possessed of ammunition and other military stores of which he stood in need. The French-Canadian *Noblesse* were the first to offer to defend the country against the invader, but Sir Guy Carleton, Commander-in-Chief of the forces, being without sufficient troops to successfully resist attack at this point, determined to retire to Quebec and make a resolute stand within its walls. He therefore dismissed to their homes the Canadians under arms, spiked the cannon and burned the *bateaux* he could not use. Three armed sloops were loaded with provisions and baggage to be ready for emergency. He felt it was a point of honour to remain at Montreal as long as possible, but it was of the utmost importance to the cause that his person should not fall into the hands of the enemy. He therefore remained until news arrived that the Americans had landed on a small island in the river, a short distance above the city,

now called Nun's Island, and then hurried arrangements were made for his departure. As he left the Château, passing out of the main entrance and down the path that led to the river, he was followed by groups of friends and citizens, whose sad countenances evinced their forebodings of the future. The historian Bouchette, whose father was one of those in attendance on the Commander, relates the incidents of the perilous and momentous journey in the following words:—

"It was through the intrepidity of a party of Canadian boatmen that the Governor of the country was enabled, after escaping the most critical perils, to reach the Capital of the Province, where his arrival is well known to have prevented the capitulation of Quebec and the surrender of the country. In reverting to the history of the Revolutionary contest, no event will be found more strikingly illustrative of the extraordinary chances of war than the perilous, though fortunate, adventure of the Commander-in-Chief of the army in Canada, whose descent by water from Montreal to Quebec was effected with safety in the very teeth of danger. The shores of the St. Lawrence for upwards of fifty miles below the city were possessed by the enemy, who had constructed armed rafts and floating batteries at the junction of the Sorel with the St. Lawrence, to cut off communication with the Capital. Upon the successful issue of so hazardous an attempt depended the preservation of Canada, and the taking of General Carleton, which appeared nearly certain, would have rendered its fate inevitable ; but the happy arrival of the Governor at Quebec at so critical a juncture, and the well-advised and active steps which he immediately adopted, secured to Britain a footing in that beautiful portion of America which circumstances threatened to forever deny her. A clandestine escape from the surrounding enemy was the only alternative left, and an experienced officer, distinguished for his intrepidity and courage, was immediately sent for to concert measures for the General's precipitate departure. Captain Bouchette, the officer selected for this purpose, then in command of an armed vessel in the harbour, and who was styled the 'wild pigeon' on account of the celerity of his movements, zealously assumed the responsible duty assigned him, suggesting at the same time the absolute necessity of the General's disguise in the costume of a Canadian peasant fisherman. This was deemed prudent as increasing the chances of escape, if, as seemed probable, they should fall in with the enemy, whose gun-boats, chiefly captures, were cruising in various parts of the river.

It was a dark and damp night in November, a light skiff with muffled paddles, manned by a few chosen men, provisioned with three biscuits each, lay alongside the waiting vessel." Under cover of the night, the disguised Governor embarked, attended by an orderly sergeant, and his devoted Aide-de-Camp, Charles Terieu de la Pérade, Sieur de Lanaudière, Seigneur de Ste. Anne, and a lineal descendant of de Ramezay. The skiff silently pushed off, the Captain frequently communicating his orders in a preconcerted manner by silently touching the shoulder or head of the man next to him, who passed on the signal to the one nearest, and so on. "Their perplexity increased as they approached the Berthier Islands, from the knowledge that the enemy had taken up strong positions at this point, especially in the islands which commanded the channel on the southwest of Lake St. Peter, which compelled their adoption of the other to the northward, although the alternative seemed equally fraught with peril, as the American troops were encamped on the banks. The most eminent danger they experienced was passing through the 'Narrows' at Berthier, the shores of which were lined by American bivouacs, whose blazing fires, reflecting far out on the surface of the waters, obliged them to stoop, cease paddling and allow themselves to drift down with the current, imitating the appearance of drifting timber frequently seen in the St. Lawrence. So near did they approach, that the Sentinel's exulting shout of 'All's well' occasionally broke upon the awful stillness of the night. Their perilous situation was increased by the constant barking of dogs that seemed to threaten them with discovery. It evidently required the greatest prudence and good fortune to escape the vigilance of an enemy thus stationed. The descent was, however, happily made by impelling the skiff smoothly along the water, and paddling with the hands for a distance of nine miles. After ascertaining that the enemy had not yet occupied Three Rivers (a point half way to Quebec), they repaired thither to recruit from their fatigue, when the whole party narrowly escaped being made prisoners by a detachment of the American Army which was then entering the town. Overcome by exhaustion, the General leaned over a table in an inner room and fell asleep. The clang of arms was presently heard in the outer passage, and soon afterward American soldiers filled the adjoining apartment to that in which the General himself was, but his disguise proved his preservation. Captain Bouchette, with peculiar self-possession and affected listlessness, walked up to the Governor, and with the greatest familiarity beckoned him away, at the same time apprising him of the threatened danger. Passing through the midst of the heedless guards, and hastening to the beach, they moved off precipitately in the skiff and reached unmolested the foot of the Richelieu Rapids, where an armed brig was fortunately found lying at anchor, which on their arrival immediately set sail with a favouring breeze for Quebec.

Arrived at the Citadel, they proceeded to the Château St. Louis, where the important services just rendered the country were generously acknowledged."

It is remarkable that the man who shared so largely in the risk involved in this dramatic scene should have been a Frenchman, Carleton's Aide-de-camp. Between him and his Chief a warm attachment continued to exist until the end of their lives, an uninterrupted correspondence being kept up between this noble soldier, Charles Terieu de Lanaudière and Lord Dorchester, after the latter with the title bestowed upon him for his success on this occasion had retired from active service in the colonies. De Lanaudière's career was a remarkable one. He began with the

Lanaudière

rank of Lieutenant in the Régiment de la Sarre, and was wounded in the battle of Ste. Foye. He was afterwards received with royal favour by King George the Third, being present at the state dinner when His

Majesty with the dignity which he knew how to assume when the occasion required, rang for the carriage of his sometime favourite, the fastidious Beau Brummel, who had presumed on his august good nature by undue familiarity.

THE CONTINENTAL ARMY IN CANADA.

ON the Sunday following Sir Guy Carleton's departure from Montreal, as the people were proceeding to church, they were thrown into a state of great alarm by the tidings of the landing of Montgomery's force on the Island of Montreal itself, at the spot where now the great Victoria Bridge springs from the shore, this densely-packed manufacturing district being then swamps and meadows. There was no hope of attempting defence under the circumstances, so both French and English, represented by an important committee of the foremost inhabitants of the town, headed by Col. Pierre Guy, entered into terms with Montgomery respecting persons and property. At nine o'clock in the morning, Nov. 13, 1775, the American troops marched in through the same gate by which Amherst had entered sixteen years before. Just inside the walls was the most sumptuous private dwelling in the city, called the Château Fortier. Its walls were hung with beautiful tapestries wrought in historical scenes, and its rooms were elegantly furnished and elaborately wainscotted. This old house still stands among the tall, business blocks, strong yet as a fortress, with high tin roof and deep windows and doors. It is now used as a tavern, but even this does not spoil the charm of its unique exterior, which still remains unchanged since the winter of 1775, when Montgomery and his officers held their mess here, and the descendants of the Puritans changed the character of the French château, as Oliver Cromwell and his "Roundheads," a century before, altered that of the English palace of Whitehall.

Little or nothing is known of what happened in Montreal during the autumn of 1775, when the Army of Congress held possession of the town. There may, and doubtless were, some sympathizers in the city who frequented the Château Fortier, but the loyalists avoided its vicinity as much as policy permitted. The French

CHATEAU FORTIER.
Where Montgomery and his officers held their mess in the winter of 1775.
COPYRIGHT.

and English ladies looked askance at the American soldiers, and if a town, invested by an enemy, indulged in any form of merriment, it is probable that no invitation was ever addressed to General Montgomery or Brigadier-General Wooster. In their rounds of the town it may have been that glimpses of home gatherings in the firelight may have given to these men of war many a twinge of homesickness for hearths across the border, where women who had been clad in satin and brocade sat spinning homespun, and were content to drink spring water from the hills, while the tea they had loved to sip in their Colonial drawing-rooms was floating about the Boston beaches. If the Boys in blue and buff encountered any of the Montreal maidens in their walks by the river, or glanced at them as they passed through the gates to wander in the maple woods around, the English girls passed them haughtily with a cold disdain in their blue eyes, and the French demoiselles flashed a fine scorn from the depths of their dark orbs, which wounded as keenly as a thrust of steel.

Events followed each other so rapidly across the line that Montgomery, tired of inaction, resolved to carry out before the year ended his cherished plan of making an assault on Quebec, and proceeded to join Arnold's men, who, half-famished and in rags, had arrived outside that city's walls.

Arnold, who was born at Norwich, Connecticut, Jan. 14, 1741, was, it is said, a very handsome man, but his character was a striking combination of contradictory qualities, and his career marked by extremes. He was the bearer of a letter from General Washington to the Canadians, in which was written: " We have taken up arms in defence of our liberty, our property, our wives and our children. The Grand American Congress has sent an army into your province, not to plunder but to protect you. To co-operate with this design I have detached Col. Arnold into your country, with a part of the Army under my command. Come then, ye generous citizens, range yourselves under the standard of general liberty, against which all the force of artifice and tyranny will never be able to prevail."

Arnold with his two regiments, numbering together about eleven hundred men, had left Boston in the month of September, with the fixed intention of penetrating the unbroken wilderness which lay between the two cities. On the twenty-second of the month he embarked with his troops on the Kennebec River, in two hundred *batteaux*, and notwithstanding "all the natural impediments, the ascent of the rapid streams, interrupted by frequent *portages*, through thick woods and swamps, in spite of accidents, the desertion of one-third of their number, difficulties and privations so great as on one occasion to compel them to kill their dogs for sustenance;" after thirty-two days of the perils of this wilderness march they came in sight of the first settlement near Quebec.

About a week later, when darkness had fallen along the river shores and lights twinkled from the little dwellings of the lower town on the opposite bank, they embarked in canoes for a silent passage across, and arrived early in the morning at Wolfe's Cove, where, sixteen years before, a similar landing had been effected, with the same purpose in view of assaulting the garrison in the seemingly impregnable fortress. For weeks the blockade was maintained, the American troops being established in every house near the walls, more especially in the vicinity of the Intendant's Palace, which once had been gorgeous with the prodigal luxury and magnificence for which this old Château had been notorious. The roughly-shod New England soldiers tramped through the rooms and up the noble staircases on which ladies of fashion had glided when the infamous Intendant Bigot had disgraced his King and office by his profligacies. These men, establishing themselves in the cupola, found it an excellent vantage point to fire upon and annoy the sentries on guard.

On the 5th of December General Montgomery arrived with his troops from

Montreal and joined Arnold. " They sent a flag of truce to General Carleton, who utterly disregarded it, declaring that he would not have any communication with rebels unless they came to claim the King's mercy."

General Montgomery, realizing that it was impossible to carry on a regular siege, with neither the engineers nor artillery requisite for the purpose, determined upon a night attack. This intention became known to the garrison, and the most careful precautions were taken against surprise. For several days those on duty and in responsible positions observed the strictest vigilance, even sleeping in their clothes, with their arms within reach, to be ready for the slightest alarm. The report reached the garrison that Montgomery had said that he would dine within the walls on Christmas Day, and he certainly seemed to consider himself sure of victory.

Arnold's communications to Carleton has been treated with contempt, no parley being entered into nor conditions considered. Montgomery tried various expedients to have his messages received, but without success, until an old woman was found willing to carry them in. On her errand becoming known, she was arrested, imprisoned for a few hours and then drummed out of the city, thus receiving the most disgraceful dismissal possible in military discipline. The two letters of which she was the bearer were directed, one to Carleton and the other to the citizens.

That to the Governor read :—

"I am at the head of troops accustomed to success, confident of the righteousness of the cause they are engaged in and inured to danger."

To the people his words were :—

"My friends and fellow subjects, 'tis with the utmost compunction I find myself reduced to measures which may overwhelm you with distress. The city in flames at this severe season, a general attack on your wretched works, defended by a more wretched garrison, the confusion, carnage and plunder which mus be the consequence of such an attack, fill me with horror ! Let me entreat you to use your endeavours to procure my peaceable admission. I have not the reproach to make my own conscience that I have not warned you of your danger."

Montgomery, waiting for a night of unusual darkness, during which he hoped to place his ladders against the barriers unnoticed by the guards, found the 31st of December suited to his purpose. On the last day of the year, when in Boston, New York and other American towns, family re-unions and festive gatherings were taking place, as far as the disturbed state of the country permitted, in a blinding snow-storm, poorly-clad, but resolute, these troops stood in line of battle, waiting for the word of command through the dreary hours of that night, in which every belfry in New England was chiming out the dawn of the New Year, which was to be the greatest in the Republic's history—1776 —the birth year of the nation.

At four o'clock in the morning two

rockets glared redly to the sky, and were immediately responded to by answering signals, which were observed from the ramparts. The solitary sentinel on St. John's Bastion reported an armed body of men approaching. It was a feint to distract attention from the point where Montgomery was to make the attack.

The tidings spread that the riflemen of New England were at the gates; the peaceable denizens of the town were startled with the cry of "To arms! To arms!" from officers hastening through the streets. The pickets in the Recollet Convent hurriedly gathered—the church bells clanged out the alarm for the troops to march at once to their posts, while drums beat and muskets rattled.

> " Ah ! then and there was hurrying to and fro,
> And gathering tears and tremblings of distress,
> And cheeks all pale—and whispering with white lips,
> 'The foe! They come, they come!'"

Lights glimmered from the frost-covered casements as fearful mothers tried to still the cries of their children, frightened with the unusual clamour. Hands were rung and tearful farewells taken of those whose duty called them out, with no certainty of return, for

> " Who could guess if ever more should meet those mutual eyes ? "

Arnold's men rushed at the barricades in Sault-au-Matelot st., with the words " Victory or Death " stuck in their hats, while Montgomery approached by a path known as " Près-de-Ville." It was extremely narrow, and obstructed with blocks of ice and snow-drifts. It was in the neighbourhood of where now are the wharves of the Allan Line Steamship Co.

In the narrowest part the Americans marched slowly and cautiously. They passed the outer barrier without resistance and approached the inner, commanded by Dambourges. All was apparently unwarned and silent, but it was not deserted. Within was a masked battery of only a few three-pounders, with a little band of Canadians, eight British Militia and nine seamen to work the guns.

The force advanced to within thirty yards, with Montgomery in front. Beside a gun, which pointed directly down their path, Sergeant Hugh McQuarters stood ready, the match in his hand lighted to send the deadly missile at the advancing column.

A quick movement—a flash—a dull boom—and the fearless leader of the assault fell dead, with twelve others, including his secretary and aide-de-camp—Arnold, his lieutenant, being wounded, and thus ended the fifth and last siege of Quebec.

It was well for Quebec that her gates that night were not thrown open to the sack of troops, among which was Aaron Burr, who had accompanied Arnold's command. These two men were possessed of less moral character than any who were connected with the Revolutionary struggle. Arnold was a strange mixture of bravery and treachery, generosity and rapacity, courage and petty spite. This arch-traitor subsequently offered to sell West Point to the British for $30,000, then took service among his country's foes, and returned to pillage and ravage his former comrades. Aaron Burr, though descended from generations of clergymen, among whom was the saintly and learned Jonathan Edwards, was guilty of murder, treason, and every other vice by which a man could become notorious, his whole career leaving dishonour, blasting, misery and death, like the trail of a venomous serpent, behind him.

Governor Carleton, being desirous of ascertaining the certainty of Montgomery's fate, sent an aide-de-camp to enquire if any of the American prisoners would identify the body. A field officer, who had commanded in Arnold's Division, consented to perform the sad office. He followed the aide-de-camp to the Près-de-Ville guard, and singled out from among the other bodies his General's remains, by the side of which lay his sword, at the same time pronouncing with the deepest emotion a glowing eulogium of the worth and character of him who, frozen stiff and cold, had been found half buried in his winding-sheet—a Canadian snow-drift. Deeply impressed by the scene and circumstances, Sir Guy Carleton ordered that his late enemy be interred in the foreign soil with the glory of martial, burial honours. In the Château Museum may be seen a sword which was picked up in the morning after Montgomery's repulse. It is in a good state of preservation, much care evidently having since been bestowed upon it.

"Of these five sieges, in the years 1629, 1690, 1759, 1760 and 1775, none were pushed with more spirit and apparent prospects of success than this blockade of the city by the two armies sent by Congress in the autumn of 1775, under the advice of the illustrious General George Washington; and, had there been a governor less firm, less wise and less conciliating than Sir Guy Carleton, the Star-Spangled Banner would now be floating from Cape Diamond.

Fort after fort, town after town, Ticonderoga, Crown Point, Saint John, Chambly, Montreal, Sorel and Three Rivers, had hoisted the white emblem of surrender, but there still streamed to the breeze the banner of St. George on the Citadel. With the black flag of rebellion over the suburbs and the American riflemen of undisputed courage and determination thundering at the gates, never had a brave little garrison to contend against greater odds, nor leader to accept a more unequal contest, no help from Britain being possible."

"When news reached Congress that the assault on Quebec had failed ; that Montgomery had been left dead on the snowy heights, and Arnold had been borne from the field ; that cold, hunger and small-pox were wasting the army, and that discipline was forgotten, the expedient was resorted to of appointing commissioners to go to Montreal to confer with Arnold, and arrange a plan for the rectification of Canadian affairs."

They were received by General Arnold in the most polite manner, conducted to the Chateau de Ramezay, the headquarters of the Continental Army, where a "genteel" company of ladies and gentlemen had assembled to welcome them, after which they supped with Arnold, probably in the dining-room adjoining the *Sâlon*.

In a vaulted cellar next to the subterranean kitchens and dungeons, Benjamin Franklin set up his printing press, the first in the city, and with it issued manifestoes to the people, to try and induce them to join in rebellion, and send delegates to the Congress at Philadelphia.

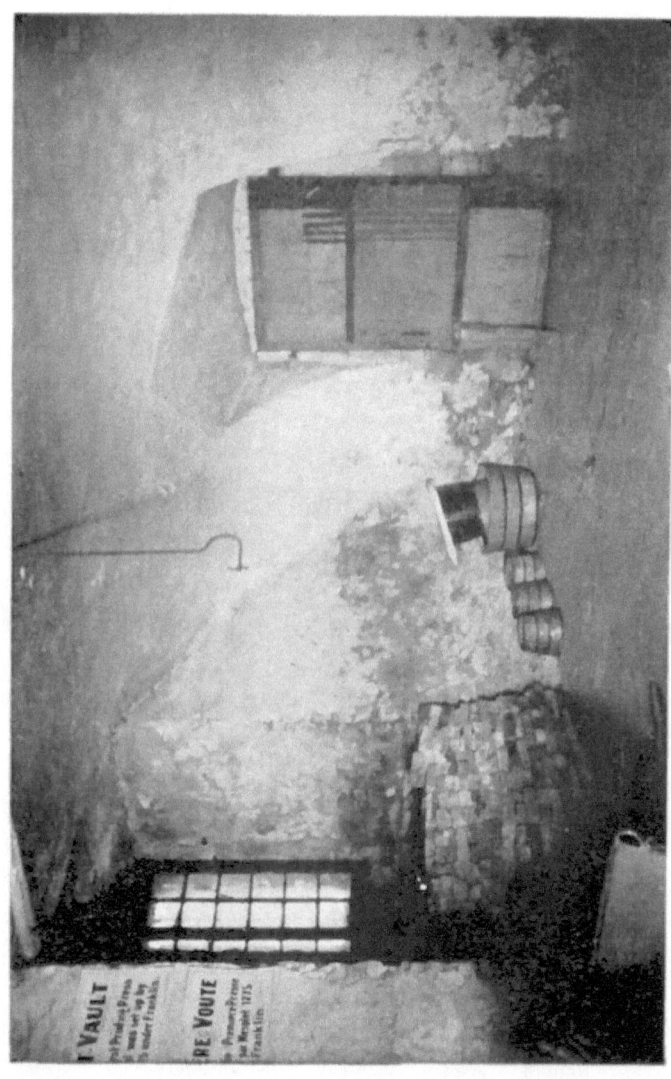

Vault in which Benjamin Franklin set up his printing press, 1775.

The instructions given to Franklin and the other members of the commission directed them to extend to the Canadians, "whom the Americans regarded as brothers," the means of assuring their own independence. They were also to demonstrate to the people of Canada the necessity of adopting decisive and prompt measures for coming under the protection of the American confederation.

Through the doors of the Château then entered Chase, Carroll, of Carrolltown (who was expected to have influence with the French people, and especially with the clergy), and others great in the young American Commonwealth's struggle for freedom. From the antiquated ovens, doubtless the brown bread and baked beans of New England succeeded the roast beef of Old England, and the *entrées, fricassées* and *pâtés* of the French *cuisine.*

In the gloom of this chamber Franklin no doubt uttered some of his wise sayings, gems of philosophy, which in his "Poor Richard's Almanac" had for years been familiar in every chimney corner of New England.

In the *Montreal Gazette*, which is still in circulation, the present voluminous and influential journalism of the Metropolis of the Dominion had here its origin in the setting up of this old hand printing-press, similar to if not the same which is now preserved in the Patent

Office at Washington. For it Franklin sometimes made his own type and ink, engraved the wood cuts, and even carried in a wheelbarrow through the streets of Philadelphia the white paper required for the printing of his paper, the *Pennsylvania Gazette*. It is now called the *Saturday Evening Post*, and has about it a certain quaintness and originality suggestive of the great mind which gave such an impetus to the American and Canadian press of over a century ago.

"For nearly one hundred and seventy years there has been hardly a week, except only when a British army held Philadelphia, when this paper has not been sent to press regularly.

His identification with the history of letters in the United States and Canada was an epoch in the development of both. In the great army of newsboys in America Franklin was the first; he was also the first editor of a monthly magazine in the country, his having on its title page the Prince of Wales' Feathers, with the motto: 'Ich Dien.'

"He has never been surpassed in the editorial faculty, at the same time being apt as compositor, pressman, verse-maker, compiler and reporter; but as adviser, satirist and humorist he was perhaps at his best. His one and two line bits of comment and wisdom were models of pithiness, and few writers have equalled him in masterly skill in argument. He is spoken of by David Hume as the first great man of letters to whom England was beholden to America."

In addition to these qualifications, he founded the Library of Philadelphia, the American post-office system, made several valuable inventions for the improvement of heating, was the first to call practical attention to ventilation, and to attempt experiment with electricity. "He founded the American Philosophical Society, and led to the foundation of the High School system in the State of Pennsylvania, assisted in opening its first hospital, and helped to defend the city against an attack of Indians. He was a leading factor in securing the union and independence of the Colonies, being the principal mover in the repeal of the Stamp Act." He made valuable meteorological discoveries, improved navigation, and was an earnest advocate of the abolition of slavery ; so that in sending Benjamin Franklin to Canada at this critical juncture, she was compelled to hold to her political convictions against one of the intellectual giants of the day. On discovering the patriotic obstinacy of the Canadians, he wrote to Congress, saying :—

"We are afraid that it will not be in our power to render our country any further service in this colony."

Perceiving the hopelessness of the situation, and that not even his matchless logic could win sympathy in his project, he left Montreal on May 11, and thus ended the efforts to coerce Canada into a struggle which was to try so sorely the energy and fortitude of the thirteen colonies— efforts which had cost them the life of one of their greatest generals—Richard Montgomery.

Franklin, when leaving, had under his escort some ladies who were returning to the United States. Of one of these he wrote to Congress, saying:—

"We left Mrs. Walker and her husband at Albany. They took such liberties in taunting us at our conduct in Canada that it came almost to a quarrel. We parted civilly, but coldly. I think they both have an excellent talent for making enemies, and I believe where they live they will never be long without them!"

Charles Carroll, who was associated with Franklin in trying to obtain the concurrence of the Canadians in revolt, was of a family which had always stood at the head of the colonial aristocracy, and which had owned the most ample estate in the country. His character was mild and pleasing, his deportment correct and faultless. By his eloquence everyone was charmed, and many were persuaded, but even his great and subtle powers in argument were abortive here. Through his daughter, Polly Carroll, he became associated afterwards with the most dignified circles of the British aristocracy. In the year 1809 two of his grand-daughters were celebrated beauties in the most exclusive social circles of Washington and Baltimore. The eldest, during a tour with her husband through Europe, formed a warm friendship with Sir Arthur Wellesley, afterwards the great Duke of Wellington. On becoming a widow and returning to London, he introduced her to his elder brother, the Marquis of Wellesley, whose wife she subsequently became. Her younger sister married Colonel Hervey, who acted as aide-de-camp to the hero of Waterloo on that momentous occasion. This family, therefore, was closely identified with that great struggle between the two nations who had fought on Canadian soil a few years before Carroll set foot upon it.

During the first Presidential court, many distinguished Frenchmen came to America; some in official capacities, others from curiosity, and many were driven into forced or voluntary exile by the French Revolution. Among these were M. de Talleyrand, the exiled Bishop of Autun, the Duke de Liancourt, the Duke de la Rochefoucauld, Louis Philippe d'Orleans and his two brothers, the Duke de Montpensier and the Count de Beaujolais.

Louis Philippe lodged in a single room over a barber's shop in Philadelphia. On one occasion, when entertaining some friends at dinner, he apologized with a courtly grace for seating one-half his guests on the side of a bed, saying he had himself occupied less comfortable places without the consolation of an agreeable company.

The exiled Prince fell in love with the beautiful Miss Bingham, the reigning belle of the city. On her royal suitor's asking her fair hand from her father, the American citizen declined the alliance with the French Prince, saying to him :— "Should you ever be restored to your hereditary position you will be too great a match for her ; if not, she is too great a match for you."

One year from the fall of Montgomery, the event was celebrated by special religious services and social functions in Quebec, the city he had never succeeded in entering. "At nine o'clock grand mass was celebrated by the Bishop in the Cathedral. On this occasion those who had shown sympathy with the Congress troops had to perform public penance. The officers of the garrison and the militia, with the British inhabitants, met

at 10 o'clock, waited upon Carleton, and then proceeded to the English Church. After the service a parade took place when a *feu de joie* was fired. Carleton himself gave a dinner to sixty people, and a public *fête* was given at seven o'clock, which ended with a ball."

About fifty years later, at Montgomery Place, on the banks of the Hudson, an aged face, with eyes dimmed with the tears of long years of waiting, looked sadly at the vessel that was bringing back to her the dust of her young soldier husband, which had so long lain in the gorge, near the fatal bastion. Forty-three years before, he had buckled on his sword to fight for what he considered a righteous cause, at the command of his leader, Washington. Expecting a speedy return, he marched away as she listened to the drum beats growing fainter and fainter in the distance, and, after half a century had passed, he was still to her the young soldier in his brave, blue coat, who had kissed her for that long farewell. All that is left on Canadian soil to recall this gallant though luckless soldier is the low-ceiled cottage where his body was laid out, a small tablet on the precipice, which reads, "Here Montgomery fell, 1775," and another of white marble, in the courtyard of the military prison in the Citadel, recently erected by two patriotic American girls in memory of the volunteers who fell with him.

One hundred New Year's Eves came and passed away, and, on Dec. 31st, 1875,

> "There was a sound of revelry by night,
> And Canada's Capital had gathered there
> Her beauty and her chivalry, and bright
> The lamps shone o'er fair women and brave men."

It was with no desire to re-kindle the rancours and strifes of that distant period, but to properly celebrate an event of such importance, and commemorate that night of blustering storm, gallant attack and sore defeat a century before, that the Centennial Montgomery Ball was given. Soldiers and citizens, in the costumes of 1775, some in the identical dress worn by their ancestors in that memorable repulse; and the ladies in toilettes of the same period, received their guests as they entered the ball-room, the approaches to which were tastefully decorated. "Half way between the dancing and receiving rooms was a grand, double staircase, the sides of which were draped with the white and golden lilies of France, our Dominion Ensign, and the Stars and Stripes of the neighbouring Republic. On the other side of the broad steps were stacks of arms and warlike implements. Facing the guests as they ascended the stairs, among the huge banners which fell gracefully about the dark musketry, and parted to right and left above the drums and trumpets, there hung from the centre a red and black pennant—the American colours of 1775. Immediately underneath was the escutcheon of the United States, on which, heavily craped, was suspended the hero's sword—the weapon by which, one hundred years before, the dead, but honoured and revered hero had beckoned on his men, and which only left his hand when he like 'a soldier fell.'

"Underneath the kindly tribute to the dead General were the solemn prayerful initials of *Requiescat in Pace*.

"At the foot of the trophy were piled two sets of old flint-lock muskets and accoutrements, and in the centre a brass cannon, which was captured from the Americans in 1775, and which bore the 'Lone Star' and the figure of an Indian —the Arms of the State of Massachusetts. This military tableau vividly recalled the troublous times of long ago, and spoke of the patience and pluck, the bravery and sturdy manhood of a bygone century.

"On the stroke of the hour of midnight, the clear, clarion notes of a trumpet thrilled all hearts present. A panel in the wainscotting of the lower dancing-room flew open as if by magic, and out jumped a jaunty little trumpeter with a slashed and decorated jacket and the busby of a hussar. The blast he blew rang in tingling echoes far and wide, and a second later the weird piping and drumming of an unfamiliar music were heard in a remote part of the barracks.

"Nearer and nearer every moment came the sharp shrill notes of the fifes and the quick detonation of the drum-stick taps. The rattle of the drums came closer and closer, when two folding-doors opened, and through them stalked in grim solemnity the 'Phantom Guard,' led by the intrepid Sergeant Hugh McQuarters.

"Regardless of the festive decorations and the bright faces around them, the 'Guard' passed through the assembly as if they were not. On through salon and passage—past ball-room and conversation parlor—they glided with measured step, and halting in front of the 'Montgomery Trophy,' paid military honours to the memento of a hero's valiant, if unsuccessful act. Upon their taking close order, the Bombardier, who personated the dead Sergeant, and who actually wore the blood-stained sword-belt of a man who was killed in the action commemorated, advanced and delivered an address to the Commander of the Quebec Garrison, of which the concluding words were :—

> 'We ask of you to pay us now one tribute,
> By firing from these heights one last salute.'

"The grave, sonorous words of the martial request were hardly uttered, ere through the darkness of the night the great cannon boomed,—a soldier's welcome and a brave man's requiem,—which caused women's hearts to throb and men's to beat exultingly." While the whole air trembled with the sullen reverberations, which echoed from crag to crag, the glare of rockets lit up the path of Près-de-Ville, as the signal lights had done one hundred winters before.

At the suggestion of the American Consul, the old house on St. Louis street, in which the body of Montgomery was laid out January 1st, 1776, was decorated with the American flag, and brilliantly illuminated, in honour of him who had so nobly tried to do what he considered his duty.

And thus the years of the century, as

they rolled around, have in a great measure smoothed away the animosities which marked those days that tried men's souls, when the sons of those who had played around the same old English hearths fought to the death for liberty or loyalty. That the angry strifes are forgotten, leaving only the memory of the bravery which distinguished the star actors in the great drama, needs no further proof than can be found on a green hill near the Palisades, in the State of New York, where one hundred and twenty years ago a warm young heart, beating beneath the soldier's red coat, was stilled by American justice. The granite shaft on the spot tells its sad and sombre story :—

> Here died, October 2nd, 1780,
> Major John André, of the British Army, who, entering the American lines on a Secret Mission to Benedict Arnold for the Surrender of West Point, was taken prisoner, tried and condemned as a spy.
> His death, though according to the stern code of war, moved even his enemies to pity, and both armies mourned the fate of one so young and so brave.
> In 1821 his remains were removed to Westminster Abbey.

A hundred years after his execution this stone was
placed above the spot where he lay, by a citizen of
the States against which he fought ; not to per-
petuate a record of strife, but in token of those
better feelings which have since united
two nations, one in race, in language and religion, with
the earnest hope that
this friendly union
will never be
broken.

" He was more unfortunate than criminal,
An accomplished man and a gallant officer."

—George Washington.

An American visitor to Quebec was recently shown the cannon used in the trophy, which the British Corporal proudly explained had been taken at Bunker Hill.

"Ah! yes, friend," the stranger replied, "you have the cannon, but we have the hill."

On the top of the monument, near Boston, which marks the spot on which this battle took place, are two guns similar to this one, the inscription on which corroborates the soldier's statement ; it reads :—

"Sacred to Liberty."

This is one of the four cannon which constituted the whole train of field artillery possessed by the British Colonies of North America, at the commencement of the War on the 19th of April, 1775. This cannon and its fellow belonged to a number of citizens of Boston.

The other two, the property of the Government of Massachusetts, were taken by the enemy.

With the failure of the American expedition, and the return of the British troops to Montreal, the Château again became Government headquarters and was called Government House.

When internal and international tranquillity were completely restored, and the people were permitted to return to their ordinary avocations of life, Sir Guy Carleton established himself at Quebec with his wife, the Lady Maria, and their three children, one of whom had been born in Canada. She had joined him at Montreal, being the bearer of the decoration of the Order of the Bath, which she had received from the hands of the King to present to her husband. Sir Guy Carleton or Lord Dorchester was one of those men " who, during a long and varied public life, lived so utterly irreproachably, that his memory remains unstained by the charge of any semblance of a vice."

On the occasion of his last appearance in an official character he arrived to make his final inspection of the troops. After general parade the officers waited upon him to pay their last respects to one who had been the bulwark of Canada through her greatest vicissitudes. The leave-taking of their old General, whom they never expected to see again, was marked by the deepest feelings of regard and regret. His connection with Canadian history covered a period marked by events of a nature the most critical, the results of which will colour the entire future of the Dominion.

Between the years eighteen thirty-seven and forty, when Canada was torn by internal rebellion, the Earl of Elgin, who was then Governor-General, drove

in hot haste to the Château, where had sat the special council during the suspension of the Constitution. After giving the Queen's sanction to what was called by a certain party "The Rebel Indemnity Bill," he rushed into one door and out of another, when this Peer of the Realm, in all the dignity of coach and four, postillions and outriders, was pelted with rotten eggs and other unpleasant missiles. Then, in the dark of night, at the instance of some so-called politicians, the mob moved on to the Parliament buildings, and, most unfortunately for Montreal, deliberately set them on fire; which act resulted ultimately in the removal of the seat of government to Ottawa and the decline of the glory of the old Château.

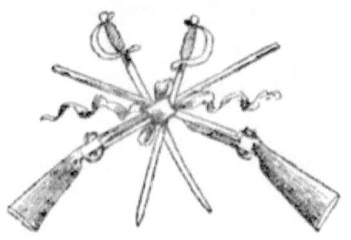

THE FUR KINGS.

IT was to the French explorers whose names stand "conspicuous on the pages of half-savage romance," and to their successors the Scotch fur-kings, that we owe much of the geographical knowledge of the northern part of the Continent. There is some uncertainty as to who was the discoverer of the Mackenzie River, which carries its waters to the ice-

Sir William Alexander

fields of Polar seas, but it bears the name of one claimant to the distinction, Sir Alexander Mackenzie.

Of the other waterways of the region much valuable information was obtained by Alexander Henry in his intercourse with the native tribes. To Sir William Alexander was given the honour of being the first Scotchman to cross the Rocky Mountains. Like his fellow countrymen, he was distinguished by the same characteristics which made their fathers in tartan and kilt foemen " worthy of any man's steel," and themselves fit successors of the bearers of such honourable names as duLuth, Joliet and de La Verandrye. A few rods from the gate of the Château de Ramezay is a tall warehouse which bears on its peaked gable the date 1793. It was in this old building that the early business years of John Jacob Astor, the New York millionaire, were spent. It was the property of the North-West Fur Company, which was the centre of so much that was romantic and captivating. This Company was an association of Scottish and Canadian merchants, who, in the political changes which had taken place, had supplanted those purely French. In energy and enterprise they did not exceed their predecessors, but had more capital and influence at their command.

In consequence of their more lavish measures, they were called the "Lordly Nor' Westers. Full justice has been done them by the pen of Washington Irving, who, in writing the tale of "Astoria," that Northwestern "Utopia," so splendid in its conception, but so lamentable in its failure, became familiar with their life in all its phases. He says:—"To behold the North-West Company in all its grandeur it was necessary to witness the annual gathering at Fort William. On these occasions might be seen the change since the unceremonious time of the old French traders, with their roystering *coureurs des bois* and *voyageurs* gaily returning from their adventurous trading in the pathless regions of the West. Then the aristocratic character of the Briton, or rather the feudal spirit of the Highlander, shone out magnificently. Every partner who had charge of an inferior post felt like the chieftain of a Highland clan. To him a visit to the grand conference at Fort William was a most important event, and he repaired thither as to a meeting of Parliament. They were wrapped in rich furs, their huge canoes being freighted with every luxury and convenience. The partners at Montreal were the lords of these occasions, as they ascended the river, like sovereigns making a progress. At Fort William an immense wooden building was the council chamber and also the banqueting hall, decorated with Indian arms and accoutrements, and with trophies of the fur trade. The great and mighty councils alternated with feasts and revels." These old days of primitive bartering are gone forever from the St. Lawrence, but to-day as it flows in majesty to the ocean, carrying with it one-third of the fresh water of the world, it is a great highway for the commerce of the globe.

The University of McGill stands on what was once, in part, the ancient village of Hochelaga, which was visited by Jacques Cartier, and was later the domain belonging to old "Burnside Hall." Its cheerful fire many a time shone out under the shadow of Mount Royal, when were gathered around its board Simon McTavish, Duncan McGillivray, Sir John Franklin and Joseph Frobisher. With them was frequently seen Thomas Douglas, Earl of Selkirk, who formulated the scheme of populating the prairies of the North-West with poverty-stricken and down-trodden tenants from older lands, many of whom lie in the old grave-yard of the Kildonan settlement on the Red River of the North, a few miles from the City of Winnipeg. Their descendants with their Scotch thrift form the backbone of that progressive province of such magnificent possibilities. Their weary journeys overland, toilsome *portages* and struggles with want and isolation are now mere matters of history, for the overflow population of the crowded centres of Europe are carried in a few days from sea to sea with every possible convenience and even luxury. The great Canadian transcontinental line has spanned the valleys and crossed the mountains, literally opening up a highway for the thousands who from the ends of the earth are yearly crowding into these vast fertile plains and sub-arctic gold fields.

Franklin lies in an unknown grave among Northern snows, lost in his attempt, at the age of sixty, to find the North Pole. He was last seen moored to an iceberg in Baffin's Bay, apparently waiting for a favourable opportunity to begin work in what is known as the Middle Sea. The problem of his fate long baffled discovery, although many an earnest searching party, in the Polar twilight, has sought him in that region of ice and snow, in a silence broken only by the howl of the arctic blast, the scream of sea-fowl or the thundering report of an ice-floe breaking away from the mainland.

One party sent out by the Hudson Bay Co. in 1853 found traces of the expedition in some bits of metal and a silver plate engraved with the name Franklin. Another, fitted out partly by Lady Franklin, and partly by public subscription, and commanded by McClintock, afterwards Sir Leopold McClintock, learned from an Eskimo woman that she had heard of a party of men, whom it was said "fell down and died as they walked." With the exception of these faint traces, their fate is still wrapped in obscurity.

INTERESTING SITES.

FEW visitors to the city, as the Palace cars of the Canadian Pacific Railway carry them into the mammoth station on Dalhousie Square, realize the historic associations which cling around this spot. In the magnificently equipped dining-room of the Company's Hotel, as delicacies from the most distant parts of the earth are laid before the traveller, he should call to remembrance the lives of deprivation and uncomplaining endurance which have made the ground now crowned by the beautiful edifice full of the most tragic interest, and filled with memories which will be immortal as long as courage and stout-heartedness are honoured.

Two hundred and fifty years ago the sound of hammer and saw here awoke the echoes of the forest. Workmen who had learned their craft in old French towns, when Colbert, the great statesman and financier, was developing the architecture and industries, revenues and resources of the kingdom, here reared a wind-mill, the first industrial building in Montreal.

The winds of those autumns long ago turned the fans and ground the seed of harvests toilsomely gathered from cornfields, among whose furrows many a time the arrow and tomahawk spilt the blood of reaper and sower. The old mill with its pastoral associations of peaceful toil in time passed away, and was succeeded by a structure dedicated to the art of war, for on the same spot stood *la Citadelle.* This stronghold, though primitive in its appointments, was important during the French occupation and evacuation of New France, being the last fortification held by French troops on Canadian soil.

This old earthen Citadel, a relic of mediæval defence, was, about seventy years ago, removed, its material being used in the leveling and enlargement of the Parade Ground, or, as it is called, the "*Champ-de-Mars.*" Its demolition might be regretted were it not that in an age of progress even sentiment must give way before advance. The grand Hotel Viger, although built to promote the comfort of the people of the Dominion, has not destroyed the pathetic interest of the early struggles and heroism which still clothes its site, and which heightens the present appreciation of a civilization of which the old mill and fort were the pioneers.

The hospitable hearth of James McGill, graced by his noble-minded French-Canadian wife, has also long since disappeared; but through his endowment, and the prince-like gifts of William Molson, Peter Redpath, Lord Strathcona and Mount Royal, Sir Wm. Macdonald and many others, the torch of education has been lighted here, which shall shine a beacon for ages to come. Although but three-quarters of a century old, yet the University of McGill compares favourably with older institutions, its Mining Building being the most perfectly fitted up in the world. Its sons take rank with the most cultured minds in Europe and America, influencing to a most marked degree the educational thought of the day.

The year 1896 marked an epoch in its history, when a graduate of the class of '68 was elected to the Presidency of the British Medical Association, one of the most august and learned corporations in the world. In calling a Canadian, Dr. T. G. Roddick, M.P., to this eminent position, a signal honour was conferred, it being the first time the office was held by a Colonial member. Thirty-five years ago, a French-Canadian youth, slight in form, with broad brow and eyes full of deep thoughtfulness, stood before the Faculty and friends as the valedictorian of his class. That slender boy is to-day the great Canadian Premier, Sir Wilfrid Laurier, the eloquent Statesman and the honoured of Her Majesty the Queen.

FAMOUS NAMES.

CONSPICUOUS among the portraits of soldiers, heroes and navigators which adorn the walls of the different rooms of the Château, is one, a full size painting of an old Highland Chief, a veritable Rhoderick Dhu, in Scotch bonnet and dirk, who, with the call of his clan, and the pipes playing the airs of his native glen, led the charge of Bunker Hill. He was Sir John Small, who came to Canada with his regiment, the famous "Black Watch," and served under Abercrombie in the battle of Carillon. One of his descendants, visiting Boston early in the century, found on the walls of a museum, and where it may still be seen, a painting of the battle of Bunker Hill with General Small on his white horse, rallying his men to the attack. It was to the credit of the successors of those who fought that day, although only thirty or forty years had elapsed since their forefathers had met in mortal combat, that the most gentle courtesy and kindness were shown on both sides by their descendants.

A fine picture of a full-blooded Indian is that of Brant, the great Mohawk Chief, an ally of the English and a cruel and ruthless foe; on one occasion having, it is said, slain with his own hand, forty-four of his enemies. Other portraits of Jacques Cartier, Champlain, Vaudreuil, Montcalm, deLevis, Dorchester, deSalaberry and Murray are also there to be seen and admired.

Many of the streets of Montreal, such as Dorchester, Sherbrooke, Wolfe, d'Youville, Jacques Cartier, Guy, Amherst, Murray, Vaudreuil, de Lagauchetière,

Olier, Mance, Longueuil, and others equally well named, will carry down to future generations the memory of those who were prominent in the making and moulding of Canada. It is strange that one of the most insignificant streets in the city, a mere lane, of a single block in

British Leader in the Battle of Bunker Hill.

length, should bear the name of Dollard, the hero of one of the most illustrious deeds recorded in history, an event which has rightly been called the Thermopylæ of Canada. The facts were as follows:— In 1660 the Colony was on the eve of extinction by the Iroquois, the whole of the tribes being on the war-path with the intention of sweeping the French from the St. Lawrence. Dollard des Ormeaux and sixteen young men of Montreal determined upon a deed which should teach the savages a lesson. They bound themselves by an oath neither to give nor take quarter. They made their wills and took the sacrament in the Chapel of the *Hôtel-Dieu*, and then started up Lake St. Louis. They were not accustomed to the management of the frail canoes of bark, and day after day struggled to pass the currents of St. Anne's, at the head of the island, where now the pleasure yacht spreads its white sails to the breezes of summer, and on whose shores the huntsmen and hounds gaily gallop when in the woods of autumn the leaves turn crimson and gold under the mellow hunter's moon. At last, after a week had been thus spent, they entered the Ottawa River, proceeding by the shores until they descried the remains of a rough palisaded fort surrounded by a small clearing. It was only a circle enclosed by trunks of trees, but here they " made their fire and slung their kettles. Being soon joined by some friendly Hurons and Algonquins they bivouacked together. Morning, noon and night they prayed, and when at sunset the long reaches of forest on the opposite shore basked peacefully in the level rays, the rapids joined their hoarse music to the notes of their evening hymn." As their young voices floated through the forest glades, and they lay down to sleep under the stars of the sweet May skies, they thought of the bells tinkling in the still air of their loved *Ville-Marie*, where those they had come to die for sent up for them *Aves* around hearth and altar. In the words of a Canadian poet, it is thus described :—

" Beside the dark Uttawa's stream, two hundred
years ago,

A wondrous feat of arms was wrought, which all the world should know.
'Tis hard to read with tearless eyes this record of the past,
It stirs our blood, and fires our souls, as with a clarion blast.
What, though beside the foaming flood untombed their ashes lie,—
All earth becomes the monument of men who nobly die.
Daulac, the Captain of the Fort, in manhood's fiery prime
Hath sworn by some immortal deed to make his name sublime,
And sixteen soldiers of the Cross, his comrades true and tried,
Have pledged their faith for life or death, all kneeling side by side.
And this their oath, on flood or field, to challenge face to face
The ruthless hordes of Iroquois,—the scourges of their race.
No quarter to accept nor grant, and loyal to the grave.
To die like martyrs for the land they'd shed their blood to save.
And now these self-devoted youths from weeping friends have passed,

And on the Fort of *Ville-Marie* each fondly
    looks his last.
Soft was the balmy air of spring in that fair
    month of May,
The wild flowers bloomed, the spring birds
    sang on many a budding spray,
When loud and high a thrilling cry dispelled
    the magic charm,
And scouts came hurrying from the woods to
    bid their comrades arm.
And bark canoes skimmed lightly down the
    torrent of the *Sault*,
Manned by three hundred dusky forms, the
    long-expected foe.
Eight days of varied horrors passed, what
    boots it now to tell
How the pale tenants of the fort heroically
    fell?
Hunger and thirst and sleeplessness, Death's
    ghastly aids, at length.
Marred and defaced their comely forms, and
    quelled their giant strength.
The end draws nigh,—they yearn to die—one
    glorious rally more
For the sake of *Ville-Marie*, and all will soon
    be o'er.
Sure of the martyr's golden crown, they shrink
    not from the Cross;

Life yielded for the land they love, they scorn
    to reckon loss.
The fort is fired, and through the flame, with
    slippery, splashing tread,
The Redmen stumble to the camp o'er ram-
    parts of the dead.
Then with set teeth and nostrils wide, Daulac,
    the dauntless, stood,
And dealt his foes remorseless blows 'mid
    blinding smoke and blood,
Till hacked and hewn, he reeled to earth, with
    proud, unconquered glance,
Dead—but immortalized by death—Leonidas
    of France;
True to their oath, his comrade knights no
    quarter basely craved,—
So died the peerless twenty-two—so Canada
    was saved.

The historian says:—" It was the enthusiasm of honour, the enthusiasm of adventure and the enthusiasm of faith. Daulac was the *Cœur-de-Lion* among the forests and savages of the New World." The names and occupations of the young men may still be read in the parish registers, the faded writing illumined by the sanctity of martyrdom. The " Lays of

Rome" recount among her heroes none of greater valour than these by the lonely rapids in the silence of the Canadian forest.

ECHOES FROM THE PAST.

NEAR a modern window in the gallery leans an old spinning-wheel, which was found in the vaults. By its hum in winter twilights, a hundred years ago, soft lullabies were crooned, and fine linen spun for dainty brides, over whose forgotten graves the blossoms of a century of summers have fallen. In hoop and farthingale they tripped over the threshold of the old church of *Notre Dame de Bonsecours*. They plighted their troth as happily before the altar of the little chapel, as do their descendants in the stately church of *Notre Dame*, with the grand organ pealing through the dim arches and groined roof.

The old, old wheel is silent, and the fingers that once held distaff and spindle have crumbled into dust, but the noble deeds and glorious names of those days gone by are carven deep in the monument of a grateful country's memory.

Over an archway in the picture gallery

is an enormous oil painting, dark with age, of the British Coat of Arms, which, it is whispered, was brought over hurriedly from New York during the American Revolution.

The museum of the Château is daily receiving donations of interesting relics, and has already a fine collection of coins, medals, old swords and historical mementoes—some of the autograph letters of Arnold, Champlain, Roberval, Vaudreuil, Amherst, Carleton, the de Ramezay family and many others, being of great interest.

These early days have passed away forever. The whirr of the spinning-wheel, or shout of the hunter, no longer sound along the banks of the St. Lawrence. No canoe of the painted warrior now glides silently by the shore; for Montreal with its three thousand inhabitants when Vaudreuil beat his retreat, to its present population of 300,000, has thrown its magnificent civilization around these spots hallowed by the footprints of the great men whose feet have walked her ancient streets.

"She has grown in her strength like a Northern
　　queen,
'Neath her crown of light and her robe of
　　snow,
And she stands in her beauty fair between
　　The Royal Mount and the river below."

The two nationalities live harmoniously side by side in commercial and social life, both retaining their racial and distinctive characteristics. The old *chansons* of Brittany are still heard from the hay-carts and by the firesides, and up and down the rivers ring out the same songs as when the "fleet of swift canoes came up all vocal with the songs of *voyageurs*, whose cadence kept time among the dipping paddles."

The Château de Ramezay has suffered many changes and modifications in the various hands through which it has passed since its foundation stones were laid, but the citizens of Montreal, revering its age and associations, are restoring it as much as possible to its original state and appearance; and the thousands who yearly pass through it testify to the romance surrounding the walls of the old Château, *Ville Marie's* grandest relic of an illustrious past—a past which belongs equally to both French and British subjects, and which has developed a patriotism well expressed in the words of the eloquent churchman, Bruchesi, Archbishop of Montreal, who says:

"I know the countries so much boasted of where the myrtles bloom, where the birds are lighter on the wing, and where gentler breezes blow. I have passed quiet days on the beach at Sorrento, where the Mediterranean rolls its blue waves to the foot of the orange tree. I have seen Genoa, the superb and radiant Florence, and Venice, the Queen of the Adriatic. More than once I have gazed upon the beauty of Naples glittering with the fires of the setting sun. I have sailed upon the azure waves of the Lake of Geneva. I have tasted the charm of our sweet France. My steps have trodden the blessed soil of Rome, and I have trembled with unspeakable gladness. But all these noble sights, all these undying memories, all this sublime poetry, all these enchantments of nature did not take the place in my heart of Canada, my Fatherland, which I have never ceased to regard with enthusiasm and admiration.

What nation can boast of a purer or more glorious origin? May the future of Canada be worthy of its noble past. May charity, true charity, reign among all our citizens as among the children of the same mother. Let us have none of those intestine divisions which enfeeble us,—none of those unhappy jealousies capable of compromising the most sacred interests."

Our fathers' battle-cries are hushed,
The ancient feuds are gone;
Canadians now and brothers,
With God we're marching on.
With spears to ploughshares beaten,
The furrowed land is won.
Through bannered fields of waving corn
In peace we're marching on.
The North wind through the pine woods
Swells out our pæan song,

To the music of its harping
We bravely march along,
And join the trampling millions,
In chorus deep and strong.
To drum-beats of a nation's heart,
We proudly march along.
O, fair, blue skies, and mountain streams
Whose flashing sands run gold,
No standard but the Triple-Cross
Thy breezes shall unfold.
With roaring surge of circling seas
We shout our patriot song
For Home and Queen and Canada,
With God we're marching on.
On, marching on, while brave the colours float
From sea to sea, with cheer and song,
This watchword pass the ranks along,
   Our Land is marching on!

www.ingramcontent.com/pod-product-compliance
Lightning Source LLC
Chambersburg PA
CBHW022008220426
43663CB00007B/1009